Parties, Parties

Gulf Publishing Company
Book Division
Houston, London, Paris, Tokyo

Parties, Parties

Fran Chiles

Parties, Parties

Library of Congress Cataloging in Publication Data
Chiles, Fran.
Parties, parties.
1. Entertaining. I. Title.
TX731.C545 1984 642'.4 83-18572
ISBN 0-87201-656-0

Art and Design by Terry J. Moore

Acknowledgments

First, to my mother who encouraged my love for cooking and entertaining, which was the beginning of this entire spiral of growing up, working, and this book. Thank you, Mother, Mrs. John J. Hafer, Sr. of Frostburg, Maryland.

If it had not been for Janet Clack Tefertiller—a marvelously talented and wonderful lady—I never would have gotten all the words and artwork together.

Nell Whaylen, my blessed assistant, has toiled literally hours with writings, corrections, typings, and editing.

Behind all these ladies there's a good man—Dave Lewis—the professional author in our group who has been our guiding light.

I would also like to acknowledge the following:

Ken Blasingame, stylist for photographs
Paul J. Daly, executive vice-president of operations, Country Club Corp. of America
Nancy and Bob Dedman, Country Club Corp. of America
Edith Deen, author
William H. Diehl, CCM, country club manager
Robert C. Floyd, chairman of the board, Fitz and Floyd
Richard Garcia, food manager, The Houston Club
Gulf Publishing Company—Clayton Umbach, Terry Moore, Leigh Owen, and Timothy W. Calk
Lynn Harris, sales planning director, Fitz and Floyd
Gary Langhammer, photography
Dale McConkey, author and consultant
Harold S. Osborne, CCM, country club manager
Win Schuler, Win Schuler Foods, Inc., Marshall, Michigan
Jimmy Parsons Designs
Charles E. Hafer, CLU
Sky Chefs, Inc.

And last, but certainly not least, all those wonderful people who make America's food the best in the world.

Contents

To my entrepreneurial, epicurean Eddie

Preface

"People frequently ask me questions about giving a party," I confided to a close friend one day.

"That's because you have all the answers," she replied. "Why don't you write a book on the subject. There's a real need, you know."

My friend was dead wrong on one count: I *don't* have all the answers. Fortunately, however, I do have *many* of them, thanks to nearly 20 years of planning and staging parties—both privately and professionally.

My friend was absolutely right on the other point, however. There *is* a need for a book on the subject, for a couple of very good reasons.

First, based on the number and different types of queries I still get about parties, I'd say most party-givers are plagued by a degree of self-doubt. They continually ask questions like, "How many people should I invite?" "What kind of wine should I serve?" "Where do I get help?" You name it, they've asked it.

Second, my research shows there's not a single definitive work out on the subject of party-giving. There are plenty of books on recipes, menus, and the culinary arts in general. But I could find none that would serve as a comprehensive handbook on party-giving.

That's why I've aimed this book at the widest possible audience—from hostess or host who wants to throw a small office or neighborhood party, to the socialite who plans to stage a glittering extravaganza, to the professional catering manager. Literally, this book is designed for *anyone* who wants to entertain in style and good taste. My purpose is to help you avoid many of the mistakes that I and many other professional party-givers have had to overcome the hard way, through trial-and-error.

The guidelines are simple and easy to follow. And they work! Use them and you'll soon be able to plan and stage just about any type party *confidently and graciously*. As a result, you'll gain a reputation as an accomplished host or hostess, able to entertain either simply or elegantly with equal success.

In Chapter 1, I explain how I use my Party Book to keep running notes on every single phase of planning—from arranging furniture, to preparing a menu, to training helpers. Post-party comments chronicle the highlights—and yes, the "lowlights"—of every single party I've held. These notes tell me what to avoid and what to repeat in planning a party.

For instance, I now studiously avoid a situation similar to the one in which a slightly inebriated kitchen helper almost ruined a perfectly delightful dinner party I was staging for the then-Governor Ronald Reagan. On the other hand, I hope to *duplicate* at some future party the ingenious seating arrangement that enabled a maximum number of guests to dine and chat with "star" guests like Tom Landry. The party honored George Strake, Republican candidate for lieutenant governor of Texas.

Chapter 2 might well be dedicated to the nation's program chairpeople—the "unsung heroes" who arrange for their clubs' meetings and parties at hotels, country clubs, and other outside facilities. I tell you whom to contact and what questions to ask to ensure a successful event.

In Chapter 3, I spell out every detail of my four-step format, or "game plan," for staging virtually any type party. You can pattern your own party from a variety of successful ones outlined in detail in this chapter.

For example, you'll read about: the brunch participants in one of our club's invitational golf tournaments (which included a surprise guest, Hollywood's James Garner); a more formal gathering for the governor of Texas; a reception for a European count and countess; a Southwest House Party (family reunion) that includes details on how to handle house guests, guest rooms, weekend menus, and a full agenda of events; and, of course, the proverbial Christmas and wedding-reception parties.

Incidentally, in my original manuscript I did not engage in "name dropping." But, I decided that readers would appreciate the fact that no one is spared crises. So, I contacted everyone and got permission to use their names.

I call Chapter 4 my "Show Biz" section. It tells you how to add a bit of razzle-dazzle and a touch of class to your party—for the most part, at minimal cost.

For example, how would you like to be able to prepare and serve such exotic-sounding dishes as flaming chateaubriand, café brulot diabolique, and banana flambé right in your own home? You *can* if you follow the simple guidelines laid down in this chapter. I also tell you how to get the most out of salads, such as a special Caesar salad, or one of my favorites: *chrysanthemum salad* for four. After reading this chapter, you'll also be able to add a dramatic flair by making your own attractive centerpieces. For instance, you can use a plain squash to prepare the eye-appealing "kissing swans" centerpiece inspired originally by Master Chef, Roberto Alaniz.

Chapter 5 deals with "fun beginnings." You'll discover how to plan and prepare hors d'oeuvres and appetizers that are certain to get your party started with a bang.

Chapter 6 gets into the "spirits" of things. It tells you everything you've always wanted to know about serving beverages. What wines do you serve with fish? With beef? These and a host of commonly asked questions about beverages are answered. You'll find out what to serve and how to serve it.

Before you get started I'd like for you to take this little quiz. It should help you pinpoint your strengths and weaknesses as a party-giver. The answers appear at the end of the quiz.

True	False	
___	___	1. *All* invitations to a party do not require a personal acceptance or regret.
___	___	2. It's proper for men to wear dark business suits and for women to wear dressy dresses for an *informal* party after 5 p.m.
___	___	3. Long sofas and large coffee tables generally provide a functional seating arrangement for your party.
___	___	4. Silver should be placed in the order it will be used, from the inside out.
___	___	5. Silver should be set uniformly, regardless of the type meal served.
___	___	6. You furnish your guests with a spoon for eating a combination of ice cream and cake.
___	___	7. Table cloths should hang 6 to 8 inches over the table.
___	___	8. All meals should be served from the guests' left with the left hand.
___	___	9. Beverages should be served from the guests' right with the left hand.
___	___	10. In organizing your party, you should plan to serve 2 to 3 drinks per person per hour.
___	___	11. Your bartender should plan to get 20 drinks per fifth of liquor, 36 drinks per quart.
___	___	12. One bartender can normally serve about 100 guests at a party.
___	___	13. In planning your party, you should allow for 10 percent "regrets."

True	False	
___	___	14. You should always order red wine with beef, white wine with fish.
___	___	15. It is improper to order wine by number rather than brand name in a fancy restaurant.
___	___	16. A major difference in red and white wines is in the percent of alcohol they contain.
___	___	17. Sherry and ports have less alcohol content than other wines.
___	___	18. All wines improve with age.
___	___	19. Guests attending a cocktail party from 6 to 8 in the evening normally make a meal of hors d'oeuvres and appetizers.
___	___	20. Flambéing is the art of cooking outside over a charcoal fire.

Answers

1. False. They *do* require prompt response.
2. True.
3. False. They are hard to get in and out of, and in addition, they create a "conversational roadblock."
4. False. From the outside in.
5. False. The menu should dictate placement.
6. True.
7. False. 12 to 13 inches.
8. False. From the left with the *right* hand.
9. False. Serve with right hand.
10. True.
11. False. It's more like 20 drinks per fifth, 26 per quart.
12. False. About half that many—50.
13. False. Usually runs about 20 percent.
14. False. Not necessarily. It's a matter of individual taste.
15. False. Head waiters usually order it from the wine bin by number; it is perfectly all right for you to do so.
16. False. Often, white wines are made with skins excluded, red wines with skins included.
17. False. Slightly *greater.*
18. False. Most red wines do. White wines are best within 2 to 6 years of being bottled.
19. True.
20. False. It's cooking with flames—*inside.*

Score:

18–20	You are probably a master host or hostess.
15–18	Not bad at all. But you need to pick up a few pointers.
10–15	Need some help.
10 or below	*Read on—hurriedly!*

HOUSEHOLD TIPS
EASY PARTY IDEAS
FRENCH COOKING
GOOD MANNERS
TEXAS FOODS
Guest List
Mr. & Mrs. R. F. Holins
Mr. & Mrs. B. F. Moore
Mr. H. H. Johnson
Mr. & Mrs. R. W. Thompson
Mr. & Mrs. W. W. Manns
Mr. John R. Bender
Mr. H. H. Redd
Mr. & Mrs. L. K. Davis
Ms. Joyce Harrison
Dr. & Mrs. C. M. Martin
Mr. & Mrs. B. W. Williams
Mr. & Mrs. L. S. Lawson
Party Notes
Date: July 10
Time: 7:30 PM
Handmade invitations
Location: Residence
Dress: Formal
Theme:

Chapter One

Planning Your Party—From A to Z

What's the main secret of staging a successful party? Without a doubt, it's *planning.* I don't mean merely jotting down who's to come and what to serve. I mean carefully—and methodically—keeping a *detailed* record of every phase of the upcoming event.

What, then is the key to successful planning? That's easy—it's a regular school notebook. That's what I use, only I convert it into what I call a Party Book, which becomes my personal diary for party giving.

I keep a detailed record of every party I give. The Party Book is my secret to organization; without it, I'd be lost.

The moment I get an idea for giving a party, I start listing details about guest lists and check lists. Later, I draw diagrams of seating and table arrangements, and make detailed food and drink lists. I list everything; I mean *everything!* By the time I've finished, I have a complete "picture" of the party I'm planning to give.

That's not all. I dutifully record all last-minute changes, and on a post-party basis, note my mistakes and ways to correct them. That's right, *mistakes!* I've made my share of them, and if you give enough parties, you'll no doubt make a few yourself. After all, most professional party-givers get that way through trial-and-error. My desire is to spare you *some* of those mistakes.

What are the benefits of keeping a detailed Party Book? Threefold, I think.

First, I feel that making a detailed book gives you confidence. If you've planned thoroughly, you can free your mind from myriad party details and concentrate on being a gracious host.

Second, the Party Book can be an invaluable ally in planning future parties. You can review your book to see *what* happened *when.* This helps you avoid duplication of effort in entertaining certain guests.

Third, the book can serve as a reminder to *avoid* mistakes you've made at past parties and to use ideas that have *worked* for you. Don't be misled. Mistakes will crop up, despite your best laid plans. Thorough planning simply helps you to better cope with them. For example, in reviewing my Party Book, I ran across a notation to "have plenty of ice on hand at all times." Why this ominous note? Because of a fund-raising party event I staged for about 100 guests. For some inexplicable reason, we decided to serve either wine or coffee, and *not* to serve water unless *requested.* The problem was, *all 100 guests requested water!* Naturally, we didn't have enough ice on hand. Needless to say, we lost our cool in more ways than one. Thus, my after-party note, *have plenty of ice available at all times!*

I suggest you keep your after-party notes religiously. They symbolize milestones en route to your becoming a truly professional party-giver.

Calming the Crisis

I can't overemphasize the need for good, solid planning, because something will almost always go wrong: the help you hired weeks ago fails to show; delivery service isn't on schedule; the guest of honor is going to be late—or worse, can't make it. You name it, I've had it happen.

So it's panic time. Right? Time to self-destruct. Absolutely wrong. It's time to draw a deep breath, tackle the problem head on, and continue as if nothing had happened. Ask yourself, "What's the worst thing that can happen if things don't go as scheduled?" I think you'll find the worst—the very worst—is that you'll have a disorganized party. But that's not likely to happen if you're prepared and in control.

In reviewing my Party Book, I ran across a number of such crises. Most were minor (and belatedly, amusing). But some were more serious (or seemed so at the moment). Perhaps the closest I came to losing my composure was when then-Governor Reagan came to dinner and was an overnight house guest in what we now call the "Reagan Room."

I asked a member of the Governor's staff what his favorite fare was for breakfast and dinner. Both were simple, easy menus. I certainly didn't want to overindulge this wonderful man when he was on such a hectic schedule. So, for breakfast we had orange juice, a slice of toast, and a soft-cooked egg, and for dinner I had planned a light consommé, followed by roast beef, vegetables, a green salad, and fruit for dessert.

The "crisis" came during dinner for four. It was a simple menu, which I had prepared myself. The reception went off like clockwork, as did the first course of the meal.

After dishes from the first course were removed, everyone anxiously awaited the second course. In fact we waited . . . and waited . . . and waited. Then, amid some increasingly nervous small talk, I heard what sounded like the dishwasher going on in the kitchen.

I excused myself and hurried into the kitchen. There I found, to my utter horror, the young lady in the kitchen reclining on the drainboard. What's more, she had taken the food off the plates and returned it to the oven.

This young lady had worked for us for some time, but had rarely cooked or served dinner. But if cooking wasn't her forte, *drinking* apparently was! She had located the cooking wine and consumed it rather liberally. Fortunately, she wasn't too tipsy to return the dinner plates and serve us immediately.

The crisis passed quickly and everything worked out fine. It usually does when you *plan* on the unexpected and remain calm.

Incidentally, I have found that for practically any type party, *everything* should be ready at least 30 minutes before your guests arrive. The candles should be burning, music playing, and the stage set before the curtain goes up. Actually, the "wrong-time" trick works well. Simply tell yourself—and everyone else in the house—that the party starts an hour earlier than it actually does. You'll find yourself ready—with time to spare.

Making guests comfortable and having a successful party is an art form, one that requires foresight and imagination. You should be prepared to meet the needs of your guests and plan accordingly. When the party starts, only the results of your planning should show—*never* the herculean effort you put into it. This concept might seem revolutionary to many dedicated culinary experts. *But I insist your planning should focus on the end product and not on excessive preparation time.* When it comes to party-giving, *planning* can spell the difference between failure and success.

Invitations and Replies

Try to send your invitations two weeks in advance. (However, one day, or even one hour is enough notice by telephone if the occasion arises, as it did with the Count and Countess de Romanones. See Chapter 3.) Invitations may be mailed, hand-delivered, or extended in person or over the phone. Let the situation dictate your method. For instance, we delivered invitations to a golf brunch to the locker room at Shady Oaks Country Club the day before the party. Reason: we decided rather suddenly to have a quick get-together before guests dashed to the airport.

Be sure to include the date (full date for souvenir), time, place, type party (or reason for having it), your name or name of the party givers, telephone number, and name for response. Put a deadline date for the response on the invitation. A name and phone number with R.S.V.P. minimizes lengthy conversation and needless return calls. Be sure someone will be available to answer the calls. Or, you may include a response card with the invitation. Be clear and precise. *All* personal invitations require a *personal* response—either acceptance or regret.

Keep your guest list, including phone numbers, in your Party Book near the phone. This is convenient for anyone who answers your phone and needs to check the responses on your list. When the response deadline passes, call the people who have not responded to make sure they've received their invitation and while you are at it solicit a reply. Another convenience in having the list in your Party Book is as a reference for future party guest lists. You can avoid repeating themes and decor with the same guests. Also, clip an example of your invitation in your Party Book for reference.

The number of acceptances you'll receive will vary with the time of year, time of party, and the local "situation." For example, in Fort Worth you can normally expect more regrets during the summer and after Christmas—probably as many as 25 percent on large parties of 100 or more. During other times of the year, regrets for these parties normally run about 18 percent. These figures probably apply elsewhere.

If you are planning a midnight buffet, say from 11 p.m. to 1 a.m., you may also reduce the food supply about 10 percent lower than the acceptances.

Because of illness or other extenuating circumstances, additional regrets will almost always come after people have accepted. This should reduce your acceptance number by an added 10 percent.

Tips on Making Invitations

Supplies for making invitations include:

1. Cartridge-type calligraphy pen
2. Water-color markers (won't bleed through paper)
3. Kneaded eraser
4. Pencils, scissors, tape, rubber cement, ruler
5. Paper—purchase to suit type of invitation; for example, use rough texture for a basket, etc.

You'll find the following suggestions helpful:

1. Check postal regulations for mailing sizes.
2. Make a practice copy first.
3. Don't be afraid to use a calligraphy pen, because it can make your handwriting fancy and pretty.
4. Be sure to pencil in guidelines lightly and erase them completely when finished.
5. Use your imagination. Remember a cleverly presented invitation is a "more inviting invitation." *Be creative!*

When you are having your design professionally printed, consider using colored paper and/or colored ink. Sometimes you can add a touch of color yourself after they are printed. Another idea is to buy your stationery with a colored border and have it printed in another color.

Tips on Making Envelopes

Supplies for making envelopes include: paper, ruler, scissors, and rubber cement or double stick tape.

Making your own envelopes adds a personal, creative touch.

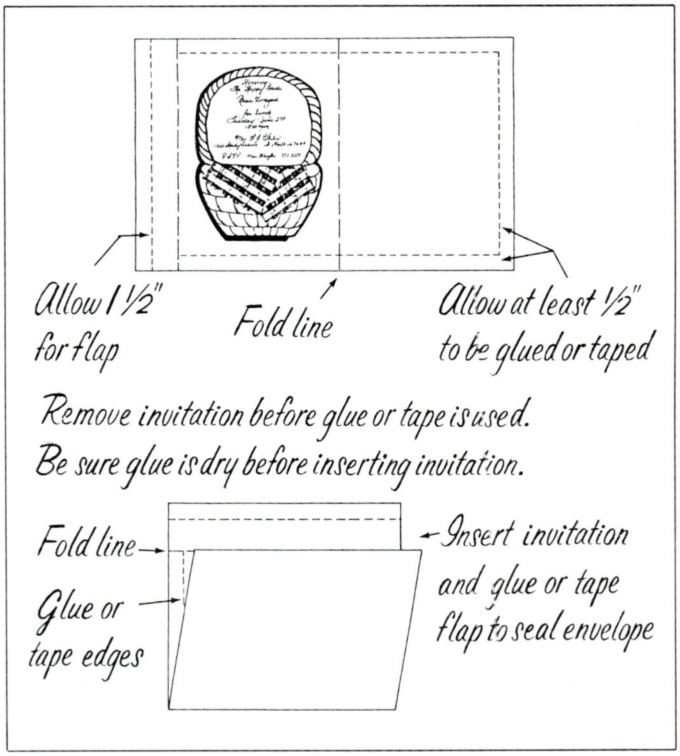

Use the same type of paper you use for invitations, and check postal regulations for sizes that can be mailed.

To make the invitation (see illustration):

1. Lay it on a sheet of paper.
2. Fold the paper over the invitation, if possible, leaving enough on one side for the flap and at least 1/2 inch on each side to be glued. (Two sheets of paper may be used, glued on 3 sides.)
3. Remove invitation before gluing or taping.

Feel free to use these invitation ideas for any of your celebrations.

Formal Invitations

These invitations are used for weddings, dances, receptions, seated dinners, state occasions, or debutante parties after 5:00 p.m. They are handwritten or engraved, on high-quality white or light cream-colored paper with black ink. They should be written in the third person and mailed two weeks in advance.

Some formal invitations and the reply requests are as follows:

An option is to use a return card, such as this:

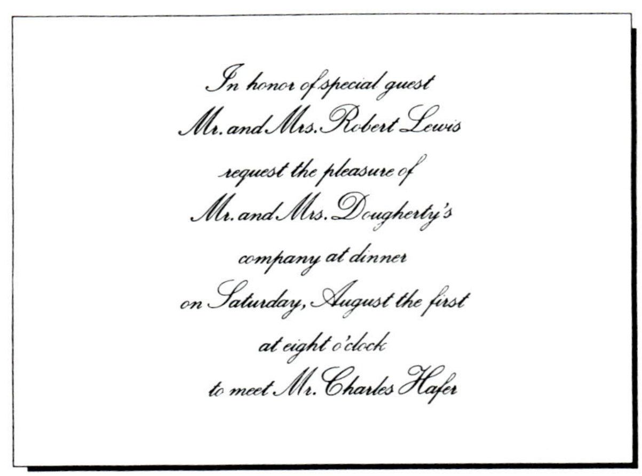

Formal replies should be on your personalized, engraved white or light cream-colored paper of high quality, or you may use plain note paper.

> Mr. and Mrs. Les Ballard
> accept with pleasure
> the kind invitation of
> Mr. and Mrs. Robert Lewis
> to dine
> on Saturday, August the first
> at eight o'clock

Or for regrets:

> Mr. and Mrs. Les Ballard
> regret exceedingly
> that because of a previous engagement
> they will be unable to accept
> Mr. and Mrs. Robert Lewis's
> kind invitation for the first of August

For more information on weddings, invitations, and etiquette, go to your local library and consult Amy Vanderbilt's *Complete Book of Etiquette.*

Formal Invitation by Telegram
MR. AND MRS. E. E. FOGELSON* REQUEST THE PLEASURE OF MR. AND MRS. JOSEPH HUMPHREY'S COMPANY AT DINNER, SATURDAY, DECEMBER TWENTY-EIGHTH AT EIGHT O'CLOCK. BLACK TIE.

Formal Reply by Telegram
MR. AND MRS. JOSEPH HUMPHREY ACCEPT WITH PLEASURE MR. AND MRS. FOGELSON'S KIND INVITATION FOR SATURDAY, DECEMBER TWENTY-EIGHTH AT EIGHT O'CLOCK.

The important items to include on your invitations are:

Who—(if honoree)
What—dinner, picnic, brunch, meeting
When—day, date and time
Where—address (and how to get there if needed)
Host or hostesses—Fran and Eddie Chiles (put lady's name first)
Reply to whom by when—If it is an out-of-town invitation, be certain to include zip code for returns or area code for phone number.

Or the invitation may say simply:

Please join us for dinner Saturday, March tenth at seven.

Susie and Jake Hill

Informal Invitations

These invitations are for any occasion. They may be engraved, printed, typewritten or handwritten, on any color paper or in any color ink. Telephone calls and telegrams are considered informal; however, if necessary, these modes may be used for a formal party when notifying the invitees it is black tie.

Informal Replies
So often the person to whom you respond needs time to assemble the guest list, find your name, and get a pencil. So don't be in too big a hurry. In replying by telephone, be sure to give information clearly and slowly.

Persons accepting calls should ask for the caller's name, and spelling if necessary. Often I ask my secretary to get correct spelling of first names so we can use them on place cards or perhaps name tags. It's usually wise to have the caller repeat the information given.

Written Reply
A card may be enclosed, as was done in the formal reply. The invitee simply fills out the card and returns it in the mail. Or, a simple note may be used.

Accepting
We are delighted to accept Saturday, the tenth at seven.

Linda Hafer

*Greer Garson

Regrets
We are very sorry we can't come on the tenth, since house guests are arriving for the weekend. (Or whatever the reason.)

Linda Hafer

All invitations should be answered as quickly as possible. This is especially important to those planning the party, at home or in another location.

What to Wear

Formal—Black tie means tuxedo with black bow tie for the gentlemen and very dressy for ladies, usually a long gown. Unless "black tie" is written on the invitation, a woman may assume a street-length dress can be worn, although engraved invitations imply formal wear.

Informal—Depends on the occasion. After 5:00 p.m. parties are generally dressy. Gentlemen wear dark business suits and ties. Ladies wear dressy dresses or their latest acquisition.

Thank-You Notes

Thank-you notes, like replies to parties, are the least you can do. My philosophy is if someone has taken the time, made the effort, spent the money to include me for their party or to send me a gift, I believe the least I can do is write them a note.

Thank-you notes are easy to write. Comment on the food, decorations, entertainment, thoughtfulness of the host or hostess, and his or her generosity. If something especially brings you joy, be sure to mention it in the note.

I recall sending a very wealthy lady zinnias when she was ill. She wrote me a note saying how especially pleased she was. They reminded her of her grandmother's garden.

Accommodating Your Guests

Once you have addressed the matter of invitations, you'll need to determine *how many* people you can accommodate at the party, and of course *where* to put them. Both factors are dictated to some degree by the occasion. For example, the number you can invite to a seated dinner will depend on seats available. Guests at a buffet dinner, or at a party where hors d'oeuvres are served, will need a place to sit and set their plate. Younger guests can sometimes find a comfortable spot on the floor.

As a rule-of-thumb, you should have a place for everyone to sit, or room in which they can stand and mingle comfortably, depending on length and type of party. Guests who have too much room won't generally mingle as readily as they do when the room is a bit crowded. Obviously, your party will "move" and be more enjoyable if the room and arrangement of furniture fits the party size and function.

So, to visualize where your guests will sit and stand, walk through your party area and take inventory. How many seats are available? At the same time, visualize where extra chairs (brought in from other rooms) might be placed.

Now, in your Party Book sketch a floor plan. Arrange all furniture—especially the bar—so that your guests can move easily from one area to another. Provide "conversational" seating arrangements.

Let's take a close look at how seating and traffic-flow go hand-in-glove.

Arranging the Furniture

Again, furniture arrangement is the key to fostering a warm and friendly environment. Believe me, I've single-handedly moved many pieces of furniture to effect this type atmosphere. And, as always, I've used my Party Book to help me figure out the best possible arrangement.

Through the years, I've compiled a brief list of furniture-arranging taboos. Chief among these are:

1. *Don't place a single chair in a corner or by itself.* Someone will end up sitting there alone; or worse, they'll have to converse with someone standing over them.
2. *Avoid huge, long sofas with long coffee tables in front of them.* This makes it difficult for the person seated in the middle to get in and out. And if they do manage to exit, it's almost impossible for them to do so

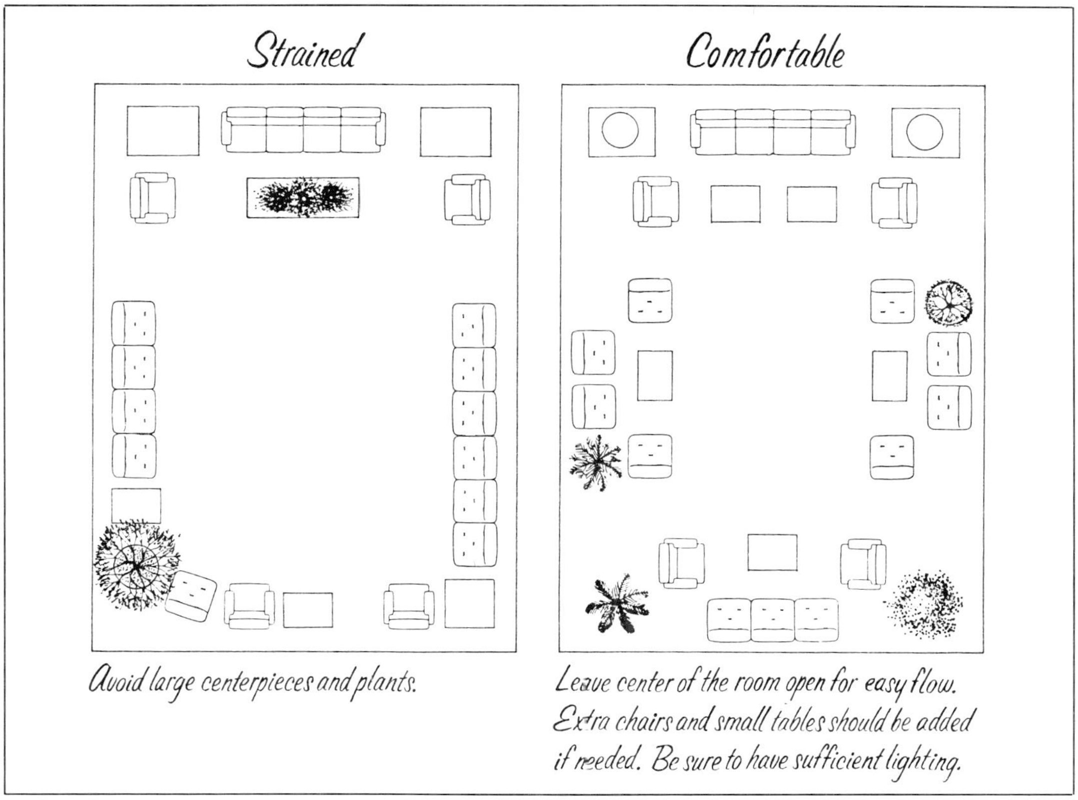

Furniture arrangement is the key to fostering a warm and friendly environment.

gracefully. They're almost certain to knock their knees against the coffee table while traversing this "obstacle course." Conversationally, the arrangement can be a disaster, too. The people seated in the middle of the couch get slightly "dizzy" talking to guests on their right, then their left.

3. *Avoid high arrangements or centerpieces.* These pieces can obstruct one's view. Playing peek-a-boo over a "beautiful" centerpiece in the living room or on the dining table can be a sure-fire conversation-killer.

My guess is that you will have to arrange your home differently for virtually every function. Eventually, your Party Book will provide you with a ready reference of all the various arrangements you have used—from picnics to formal dinners.

Accordingly, you'll want to write "remember notes" in your Party Book after every party or meeting so you can continue to improve your planning. If something goes wrong, make a note. And by all means keep detailed notes on everything that goes *right!*

Keep the Traffic Flowing

Because it normally gets so much traffic, the bar is usually a key factor to consider in creating traffic flow patterns. In fact, your bar will usually *control* the traffic pattern at your party.

"Coffee, tea, or . . . " You'll want to direct your guests to the serve-yourself area upon arrival. But be sure to have all your refreshments ready. Your bar may also be a non-alcoholic beverage station for fruit juices or punch.

You may use bartenders or have guests serve themselves. The size and nature of your party usually dictates the preference.

One advantage of self-service is that it makes your guests feel at home. In addition, it provides a certain "anonymity" for those who don't want you to know what they're drinking. The reverse may be that you don't want to "advertise" the brands you are serving. In any case, the self-service arrangement proves best for small parties.

Be as specific as possible in locating your bar. It'll help you avoid crowds, bottlenecks, and disenchanted guests. And since you may have to replenish your bar *frequently* during the party be sure to have ample reserves nearby.

In serving cocktails, I have found one arrangement that works quite successfully: I simply separate the wine table or non-alcoholic beverages from the bar, usually placing them on opposite sides of the room.

In this setup, wine can be already poured in wine glasses. Additional wine in buckets adds a nice, aesthetic touch to the table arrangement. This arrangement is helpful for a couple of reasons. First, it cuts down traffic at the bar, expediting the serving of drinks for everyone. Second, some people, especially ladies, feel more comfortable picking up a glass of wine on their own rather than "ordering" from the bar. Instead of wine, or in addition to it, you may want to serve spiced tea (see recipe in Chapter 6).

Placing a wine or hors d'oeuvre table away from the bar will probably give you an even distribution of people and keep the "traffic" flowing smoothly. Separate the food stations from your beverage set up.

Meetings with Speakers

Special furniture arrangements are usually required for meetings, such as your church social, that center around a speaker. In these cases, the needs of the speaker (and often the president and officers of the organization) are paramount.

I always try to query these people in advance to see what their special needs are. Generally, you'll want to place the speaker in a well-lighted area where he can be seen, as well as see his notes.

I usually follow this checklist in preparing for a meeting that spotlights a speaker:

1. Is a podium—or something—available for the speaker's notes?
2. Is the speaker using visual aids, such as an overhead or carousel projector? If so, is there an electrical outlet nearby? Have an extra projector bulb available in case the one he is using burns out. And by all means, don't forget to have an extension cord available.
3. Have water and glasses available for the speaker.
4. Provide a table for the projector; appoint someone to handle the lights if necessary.
5. Provide audience members materials for writing—and tables to write on. Provide extra paper, pencils, scissors.
6. Provide protection pads for your tables.
7. Provide napkins, and a place for cups and plates.
8. Make name tags available.
9. Are there enough chairs? You might have to rent or borrow a few.
10. Turn the telephone off in the meeting room.
11. Don't forget to put your pets outdoors.
12. Put a note on your doorbell that says, "Open, come in," if you don't have someone to greet each guest. Also, this helps latecomers.

It's usually wise to assign special responsibilities to some guests or a close friend. People like to participate and be involved. Give them a rundown on the agenda of your meeting. And make a special effort to put someone in charge of introducing various people and giving a warm welcome.

Greeting and Seating Your Guests

One of the most critical parts of the planning process is to determine who your guests will be and how you will accommodate them. Again, the idea is to keep your guests' interests at heart *at all times.*

When your guests arrive, they'll naturally need adequate parking facilities. If it's formal or a very large affair, you might make car parkers available; umbrellas, too, if the weather looks bad.

A warm greeting at the front door is a *must.* You may greet guests yourself or delegate the role to a gregarious friend if possible. In any case, guests should *always* be greeted warmly.

Once inside, your guests will need some place to put their coats, purses, and umbrellas. You can designate an area and let guests handle this matter themselves. Or, you might want to assign this task to someone. If you have a special guest or speaker, place him or her in the receiving line, or be sure someone is responsible for seeing that he or she is introduced to other guests. Otherwise, these special people won't know what they are expected to do and your guests will lose the opportunity to meet the honoree.

You'll normally want to have a table available for name tags near the entrance. Ashtrays and trash receptacles should be strategically placed. If it's a business meeting, you may want to set up a card table or TV stand for name tags and literature, and possibly a guest book. If it is a political meeting, have bumper stickers, volunteer cards, and voter registrations available.

Who's to sit with whom is a perennial dilemma, but one you must work with constantly. Certainly it's a matter over which you will want to exercise at least limited control. Otherwise, as most of you probably realize, guests will tend to sit with the same familiar groups.

I know that Eddie and I find ourselves seated with the same people at any number of social functions. And like many couples in similar circumstances, we've pretty well covered the waterfront conversationally. As a result, we find most of our friends are generally agreeable to sitting with less familiar couples and striking up new relationships.

I strongly suggest that you *creatively* seek ways to "mix" your guests for maximum enjoyment. True, it's a challenging and time-consuming task, but one that is worth the effort.

I like to use place cards. This is the simplest and most direct way to put people where you feel they're most likely to enjoy themselves Essentially, I try to place guests with people they don't know too well, but with whom they appear to have a great deal in common.

When I can, I give widow guests preferential treatment. I try to place them with males and young people. They tend to welcome masculine conversation and want to avoid being the "lady-on-the-shelf."

Always look for ways to get maximum "mileage" out of celebrities and other special guests. I think we did this rather successfully at a recent party honoring Annette and George Strake, candidate for lieutenant governor of Texas, and Cynthia and State Senator Mike Richards, candidate for state controller of Texas. Our co-hosts were Corky and Bayard Friedman, chairman of the board of Texas American Bank-Fort Worth (formerly Fort Worth National Bank), and Mary Frances and Bill Conner, co-founder of Alcon Laboratories. Because our honorees were politicos who were running in statewide races, we naturally tried to get them maximum exposure.

Special guests at this party for 80 were Dallas Cowboys' Coach Tom Landry and his wife Alicia, and Tarrant County Republican Party Chairman Charles Lundelius and his wife Lynn.

Realizing that most guests would like to get some "confidential" Cowboy scuttlebutt from Coach Landry, we gave him, and other honored guests and co-hosts, "star" status. Then we came up with a rather ingenious way for many of our guests to "share" them.

These stars were given name tags with a number written in the corner of each tag. This number corresponded to a number in the center of the dinner table. (Only stars had place cards.)

Stars, co-hosts, and special guests were then scattered strategically at different tables. Each table seated 10 people. We dispersed the couples as well, asking them to sit at a table different from their spouse's.

After the regular meal and before dessert was served, we asked the stars to move to another table. The number of the table to which each one was to move was written on his place card.

The result (and it was a very happy one) was that more people got to visit with our honorees, co-hosts, and stars. For instance, since there were 10 people at each table, both Alicia and Tom Landry sat at two tables each, giving a total of 36 people the pleasure of dining with the Landrys and the other stars. It was exciting, and we received a number of favorable comments about the arrangement.

Serving Your Guests

Now to the challenging task of what to serve your guests. My secret philosophy for preparing food is simple. Generally, try not to prepare anything that takes longer to fix than it does to eat, and it must be eye appealing.

Naturally, it isn't always possible to follow this principle. For example, it often takes me at least an hour to fix a cold meal for my husband's dinner; it takes him only eight minutes to eat it!

So generally, I concentrate on the final product and not lengthy, time-consuming preparation. After all, it's not how much time you spend in the kitchen that counts, it's how the food looks and tastes, and how much fun your guests have.

What kind of food should you serve? Choose food that suits the occasion. Usually, you'll want to serve light and dainty foods for teas and ladies' gatherings. For outdoor activities and when men are invited you'll probably want a more substantial menu.

The rule-of-thumb I invariably try to follow is: cater to your guests. Consider their unique preferences and desires.

Generally, I've found, out-of-town guests are interested in *local* foods and life styles. For example, I recently attended a party honoring an Italian celebrity. The motif—and the food—was strictly Italian. The Italian gentleman confided to me later that he would have preferred a Texas barbecue, which he had heard a great deal about but hadn't tasted.

Incidentally, one of our most successful parties was a real Texas barbecue for the chairman of the board of Manufacturers Hanover Trust Co., John McGillicuddy. The Easterners loved it. After all, it's something they don't routinely get in the Big Apple.

Nutrition is a vital concern *always!* As a thoughtful and gracious hostess, it's not only *necessary,* but *kind* to give careful consideration to your guests' health. Keep in mind the basic four food categories that have remained unchanged through years of diets and food fads. The FFB or *F*our *F*eel *B*etter Groups are:

1. Meats, poultry, fish, and beans
2. Dairy products
3. Vegetables and fruits
4. Whole grains, cereals, and breads

It is necessary, of course, to feed your guests nutritionally. It is even more important to *avoid excesses.* The main villains have been—and still are—sugar, fat, salt, caffeine, and poor eating choices. Please don't offer excessive calories to your guests—be it food or alcohol. I mean this. I promise you I will eat the parsley off the hors d'oeuvre tray before I'll touch those pretty, puffy, pound producers.

My husband, the most important person for whom I prepare meals, always gets simple nutritional entrees. Lean meat, poultry, or fish, fresh vegetables and salads make up most of our meals.

We wouldn't know what a roll or rich dessert was if we didn't eat out occasionally. By serving such foods, you are literally inviting your guests to join the FFS—the *F*uture *F*at *S*quad. Or, to put it another way: try to minimize *F*ats, *F*lour, and *S*ugar.

Simple foods, simply prepared, reduce your preparation time and enhance health. Please realize this is a guide that will enable you to begin entertaining with more enthusiasm and confidence, eliminating stress and disappointments.

Keep these valuable tips in mind as you write out your menu or refreshment selections in your Party Book:

1. Plan your menu to coordinate with your favorite silver, china, linens, glasses, etc.
2. Make foods easy to serve with minimum effort, ensuring easy flow of production and handling. Don't have too many courses and avoid last-minute preparations. The more items you have, the higher the risk of quality-loss and crisis.
3. Plan not to "stuff" your guests. (Spare them from immediate fasting, guilt feelings, and increasing physical discomfort when they depart.) Carefully avoid thickening agents and heavy grease preparation methods. I will even go so far as to confide that I minimize buying such items as cornstarch, flour, and other carbohydrate mixes known in the trade as "fillers" or "risers." I do not wish to puff up, paste on, or push out my own body, nor my guests'.
4. Use bright colors, different textures, and interesting shapes. Red food, red garnishes,

and red accessories are my favorites. Since so many china patterns and foods are bland and subdued in color, red is aesthetically pleasing and adds excitement and overall enchantment. Avoid repetition in foods and garnishes on the same menu. Maraschino cherries are greatly overused for the Shirley Temple beverage, fruit appetizer, fruit salad, and the parfait. Parsley comes in second for overuse.

5. Prepare food that's easy to eat. Keep it *bite-size,* including fruits and greens in salads. Avoid dripping items. Do not serve meat that contains bones and is difficult to eat, except at picnics.
6. *Always* be ready for more guests, even at small, seated dinner parties. There are invariably those last-minute can't-come or may-I-bring-a-friend accommodations. This is a fact of life, so include it in your planning. This way, you'll be "delighted by extras" and not "frustrated by dropouts." It happens all the time. For example, I had such a crisis arise recently. After two of the guests declined an invitation, I changed the table and place settings to accommodate fewer people. As fate would have it, the two who had "declined" arrived at the party right on time. I simply added two places and made some smaller servings on the plates. To make the plates more attractive, I added garnishes. No one ever knew, and things went smoothly.

Creating a Mood

Scented candles, soft music, flowers . . . these are the little touches that can make your party a romantic, memorable experience. Here are some proven tips for creating such an atmosphere and ensuring the comfort of your guests:

1. Use soft-light bulbs to provide mood and atmosphere. We all look better; it doesn't drain facial color. Pink bulbs are great. Keep lights dim—not bright.
2. Soft music promotes a relaxing atmosphere. Loud, fast music encourages guests to hurry, causes tenseness, and discourages genuine and effective communication.
3. Pleasantly scented candles, never overpowering, enhance the environment.
4. Use only one or two major colors throughout your theme, or decor, for maximum effect.
5. Name tags help a party to be more enjoyable. Let everyone write his or her own as they enter. Have each one write one or two things that are of interest to them on their name tag. (For example: I'm from Maryland, or I'm a Texas Ranger Fan.) This encourages conversation. Of course, you can have name tags done ahead of time and carry out the theme of the party.
6. Have the room temperature cooler than normal.
7. Be sure the size of the floral arrangement is suitable. Often floral arrangements and party designs are made to make an overall impression. But when they obstruct vision, conversation, and maximum comfort, they are too large.
8. Omit candles on the table unless you light them. Avoid candles flickering at eye level or candleholders that obstruct views. Since I love scented candles, I use them for their pleasant fragrance. I use them anytime—especially during Christmas holidays. Use votives or floating candles as an alternative. If tapers are used, it is proper to use at least four, for a formal dinner. Beware of flames flickering at eye level.
9. If "everyone is doing it," it's time for a change. Be different, individual, original, and creative.
10. After the party, use your flowers to make others happy. Often, my husband's dressing area is flower-scented for weeks from "leftover" party flowers. Also, you can share your flowers with neighbors, special guests, or hospital patients. Save the petals and let them dry for a potpourri.

In your Party Book, include a check list for *final touches.* These are the things you think of early, but want to be sure they are done just before guests arrive. Here are some suggestions:

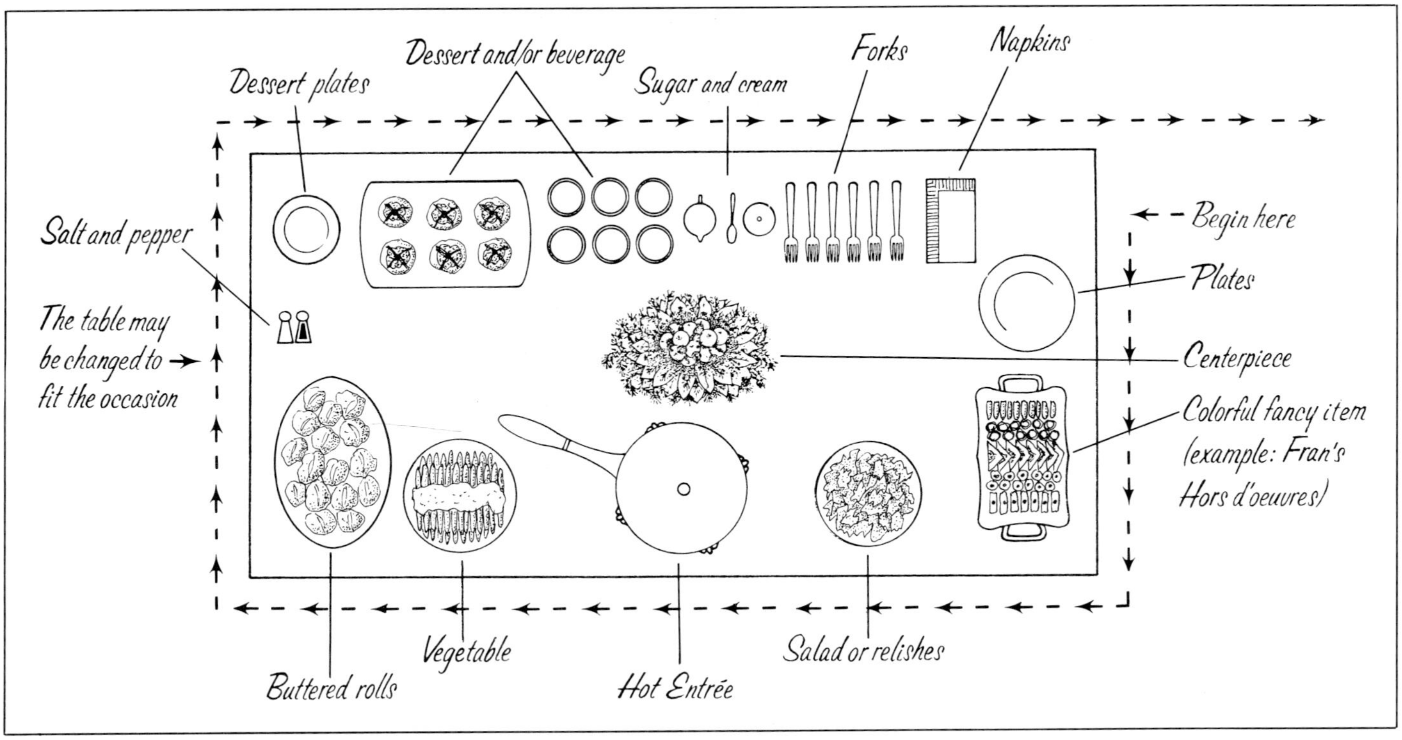

Arrange your buffet table so that guests pick up items in a logical sequence.

1. Light candles—adjust lighting.
2. Properly adjust drapes and blinds.
3. Play music.
4. Double check restrooms.
5. Adjust room temperature.
6. If possible, turn the telephone bell off. At least, turn it down, especially if you are having a meeting.
7. If smoking is allowed, provide plenty of ashtrays and matches.

Planning Table Settings

Correct functional table settings are important. In your Party Book, sketch and plan your table setting to suit your party needs.

Buffet

Buffet-style serving is fun. If guests outnumber the places at your dining table, set up card tables or small tray tables. Place settings may be set up ahead of time, or you may be casual and let your guests sit where they choose. For a buffet, you can be fancy and use your best china, or keep it casual with simple accessories. It's up to you.

Imagine yourself going through the buffet line and picking up items in a logical sequence. Arrange the food attractively, placing the most colorful items as focal points. Place serving dishes so guests can easily serve themselves. Include serving fork or spoon with each item.

Decide how many forks, spoons, plates, and cups you'll need and put at least that number or prepare for handy refills so as not to crowd your table.

You may want to consider some of the following options for a buffet:

1. Set silver, salt and pepper, napkins, beverage on individual tables ahead of time. Or, roll silver in napkin for easy pick up. Note: Silver at the end of the line is more convenient for guest.
2. Set separate serving area for guests to pick up the items in No. 1.
3. Set separate beverage station.
4. Set separate dessert station.
5. Serve salad, rolls, dessert or any course separately.

Place setting identification chart.

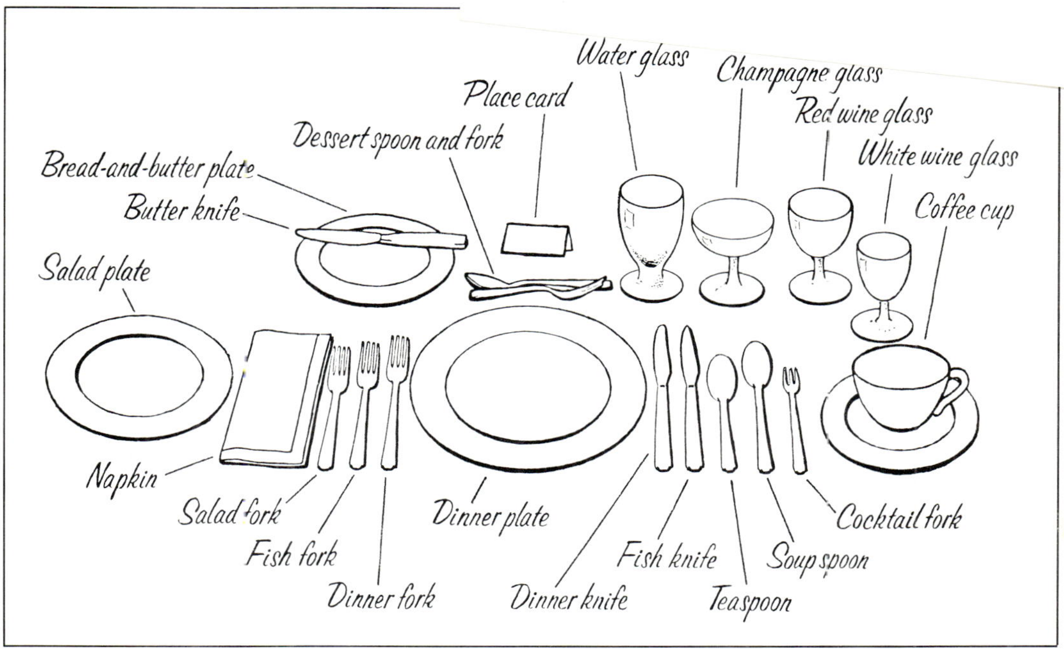

Seated Dinner

A seated meal menu may consist of seafood, first course, entree, salad, dessert, coffee with dessert or after dinner. The table setting shows how to set a table for this menu with the option to serve silverware with dessert. The cups for coffee can be served at this time also.

Silver is placed in the order it will be used from the outside in on both sides of the plate. Silver that is not needed should not be placed on the table. Knives and spoons go to the right of the plate, with each knife's edge facing the plate. A bouillon or soup spoon is at the extreme right, with the cocktail fork to the right of it. Other forks are to the left of the plate, from outside in: salad fork, fish fork, and meat fork. (Note: fish

In this table setting the china, chairs, flowers, and table cloths are color coordinated. Note: Sit down at the table to make sure everyone can easily see over the centerpiece.

frequently.) Depending
be salad fork, meat or
sert fork. It is best to have
le before the guest is seated,
p or dessert courses with which
e the silver. Another thing to
s the hostess takes the first bite of
se and the guest follows accordingly.
glasses are also placed in order of use
the first being nearest the guest's reach.
esumably, the white wine first, red wine next,
and champagne or sweet wine with dessert.

Service plates, when used, are in front of guests at all times, except when the main course is served at formal occasions. This requires professional help, and because my emphasis is on the more casual life-style in today's world, the information here will provide you with correct and proper service without the need for extra help for any occasion.

Dessert

Desserts may be served to guests with either dessert spoon or fork on the dessert plate. Or, the dessert silver may be placed at the top of the plate, which facilitates service when help is limited or when serving is done by the hostess.

It is proper to place one utensil on the dessert plate rather than have your guest juggling two utensils, such as the spoon and fork. If you are serving ice cream and cake together, use a spoon. If you don't have enough silver available, simply resort to a quick wash between courses.

Other Seated Dinner Tips

Line up silver and plate about 1½ to 2 inches from the table edge; allow 24 inches from plate center to plate center per person. Lace or linen table cloths should drop 12 to 13 inches over the edge of table for a formal dinner; white linen placemats are acceptable.

Water and wine glasses are placed above the knife and spoon. (Water glass at the top of the knife, wine glasses to the right in order of use.) Never place glasses or cups on table turned upside down, nor should a guest perform this action. "No thank you" is sufficient.

Basic Rules for Food Service

As the saying goes, good help is hard to find these days. So, I suggest you do everything in your power to enlist—and train—competent help.

Where do you look for help (kitchen help, waiters, bartenders, parkers, caterers)? Mostly in country clubs, restaurants, hotels, military bases, colleges, high schools, and referrals from your present help. Often, you can get help by calling the headwaiter, hostess, catering manager, or owner of your favorite local restaurant or club. They generally are happy to offer competent advice.

When you hire help for your party, ask up front what they charge. Pay rates vary from minimum wage, plus transportation costs, to flat rates for services. Also, be specific about dress, arrival, and approximate departure time. I request black pants or skirts, white shirts or blouses, black bow tie and black jackets for men. Clearly spell out all duties and be specific about your expectations, including the how-to-clean-up detail after the party. For your own sanity, I suggest you emphasize that they are to have the party and kitchen areas back to normal *before any of your helpers leave.* Everyone should work together to the end.

Always pay helpers when they have completed their duties—not later. Prepare individual pay envelopes ahead of time or have checks made out and ready.

To ensure that your helpers observe proper party protocol, I suggest you go over each of the following basic rules for food service with them. These rules are to be followed except when guests' comfort dictates otherwise. After discussing each of the basic rules thoroughly, post the rules on a board or door in the kitchen, where all the helpers can readily see them. It'll be a constant memory-jogger. Also, post the menu, along with a time schedule and duties, in the kitchen. Remember, show time begins at least 1 hour before the guests arrive. So, post notes on your menu for approximate serving times, especially hors d'oeuvres, beverages, and the like.

To help reduce the possibility of last-minute errors. indicate to whom and/or where each item is to be served; for example, "Living room, before dinner," or "Patio table, with after-dinner champagne."

1. All food is served and dishes removed from the guests' left, with the left hand. Avoid reaching in front of guest.
2. All beverages are served and removed from the guests' right, with the right hand.
3. Serve ladies first and the hostess last before serving men.
4. Never pick up a glass with your hand over its top.
5. Try not to remove coffee cup or glasses from the table for refill.
6. Keep napkin in left hand to wipe drip from coffee pot or water pitcher.
7. Never stack or scrape plates in front of a guest.
8. Remove salt, pepper, butter, and excess silver after main course is cleared.
9. Handle spills or accidents quietly, quickly and without further embarrassment to guests or employees.
10. Avoid carving meat in the dining room. This procedure is time-consuming and messy. Other foods might get cold. Every plate fixed in the kitchen ensures a better end product.
11. It always facilitates the service to set up a beverage station as near the serving area as possible. (Cups, saucers, glasses, ice, water, lemon, sugar, coffee, decaffeinated coffee, tea, hot water, etc.)
12. For buffet service, one should always have an overseer to ensure guests move through the line easily and that refills are adequate.

Again, I remind you: the best trained staff makes mistakes. So do not fall off your chair, faint or act indignantly when one occurs. Just be calm and carry on like, "Doesn't this happen to everyone?" *Believe me, it does!*

Chapter Two

Planning Parties at Hotels and Commercial Facilities

You're a newly appointed program chairman of your local business or professional club, and your job is to plan a meeting or party at a commercial establishment.

"Great," you're likely to think, "I can turn the job over to the professional party-planners at the hotel and they'll take care of *all* the details."

You'd be right in one sense. You *can* turn the job over to a competent pro and normally expect a turnkey job. By and large, these people are capable, dedicated professionals. But you ordinarily should not assume that your expectations would be carried out by the professionals in a commercial establishment as you would handle your own party at home.

First, on certain occasions—and for varying reasons—commercial establishments' staffs are sometimes either understaffed or overloaded with work. Under these circumstances, you may not get the specialized attention you desire.

Second, as competent and well-trained as these managers are, often their staffs do not know your expectations or personal desires. The staffs of commercial enterprises, although very people-intensive, are from varying backgrounds and communications are often impaired.

Third, just as *your* best-laid party plans sometimes go awry, so do the commercial establishment's. Crises will happen, even at the plushest and best-run commercial establishments. (Incidentally, a commercial establishment can be a hotel, town hall, cafe or restaurant, convention center, private club, or similar facility.)

So what does all this mean to you as program chairman or club leader? It means you need to plan for a party at a commercial establishment every bit as diligently as you would for a party in your own home. Only at the commercial establishment, you plan *through* someone else, typically a catering manager, or food and beverage manager. These are the people to whom you delegate responsibility for running your party.

Like any good delegator, however, you'll need to keep tabs on how things are going. I get best results by checking periodically *before* the meeting or party to make sure everything is in place, and by *being on hand* just before and during the meeting to make sure everything is going smoothly. The planning needs and follow-up are basically the same, whether you're holding the party at home or at a commercial establishment. So, if you want to impress your boss or club members with the "party-of-the-year," get your Party Book and start writing.

The first step in planning your event is to make an appointment with the commercial establishment's catering manager (or whoever is in charge). Make sure you write down his name, the name of the facility, street address, and phone numbers. You'll need this information in writing correspondence and sending invitations. It will also probably be used in dealing with those who handle decorations, flowers, entertainment, billing, and the like.

In this initial planning session, you should review with the catering manager virtually every aspect of the party—from seating arrangement to cost. But before getting down to brass tacks about these details, spend as much time as you can establishing rapport with the people you'll be dealing with at the commercial establishment. The reason for this should be obvious. The better you understand and work with each other, the more satisfying the results are likely to be.

Generally, the guidelines you followed for holding a party or meeting in your own home apply to hosting an event outside of it. The primary differences are that you are delegating responsibility for the party to others, and in most cases you are obligated to follow certain "house rules."

Here are the topics I discuss—and the approach I usually take—in the first planning session:

Facilities

Right away, take a close look at physical facilities to make sure they suit your needs. If there's a question in your mind about the room being inadequate (too small or too big, poorly lighted or ventilated, or undesirable location), *request* a more elegant, practical or commodious meeting place. The meeting place can help create the proper "atmosphere," which can sometimes make or break a meeting or party. Just as in planning a meeting in your own home, *guest comfort is the prime consideration.*

Seating

If the meeting room passes muster, start talking about furniture arrangement. How many tables and chairs will be needed? How will they be arranged—theater style or conference style? Request a floor plan showing your room arrangement and table numbers if needed. This is necessary if you're taking reservations for tables. Generally, theater style is preferable when the speaker is to hold forth most of the time. Conference-style seating is generally more effective when extensive audience participation is anticipated.

Here are some general diagrams and guidelines for seating:

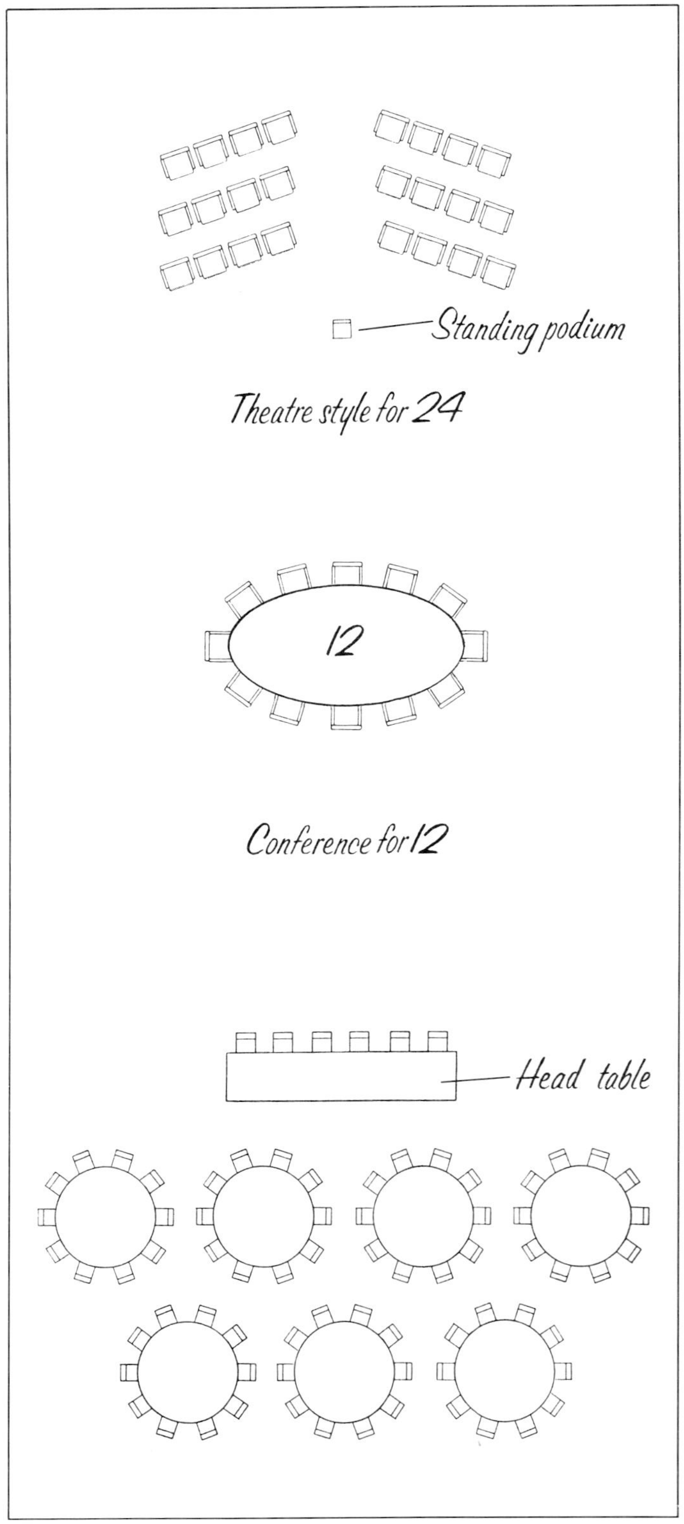

The number of persons attending will often dictate the seating arrangement.

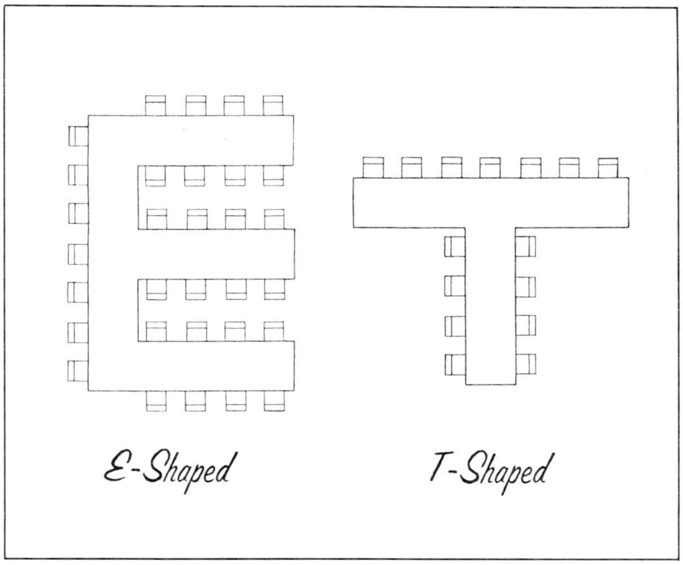

Not recommended.

E-shaped and T-shaped tables are very awkward from a conversation standpoint. It is better to use individual tables of 8 or 10 and have a designated "head table" for honorees, or if necessary a U-shaped table.

Arm chairs require additional room. Seating space at the tables can vary from 18 inches (minimum) to 24 inches (preferable). Table cloths should drop 12 to 13 inches from the table edge. The exception is that drapes for head tables or banquet tables should be longer or floor length.

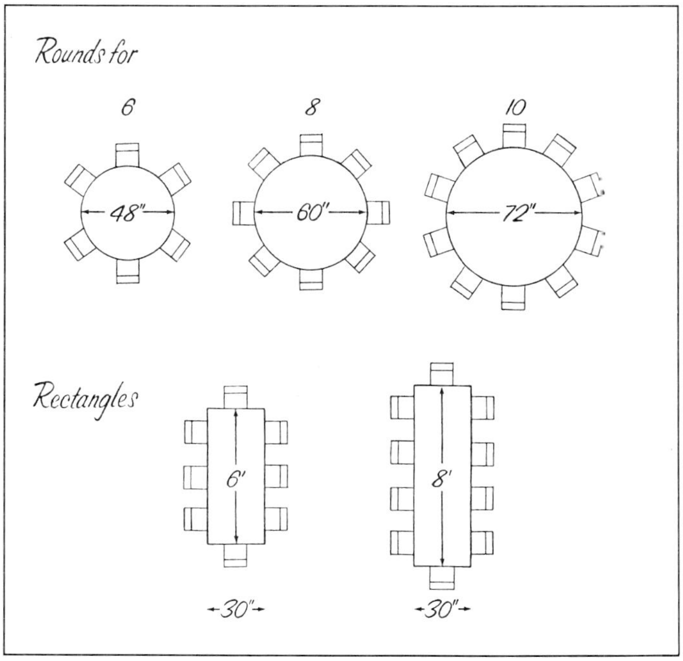

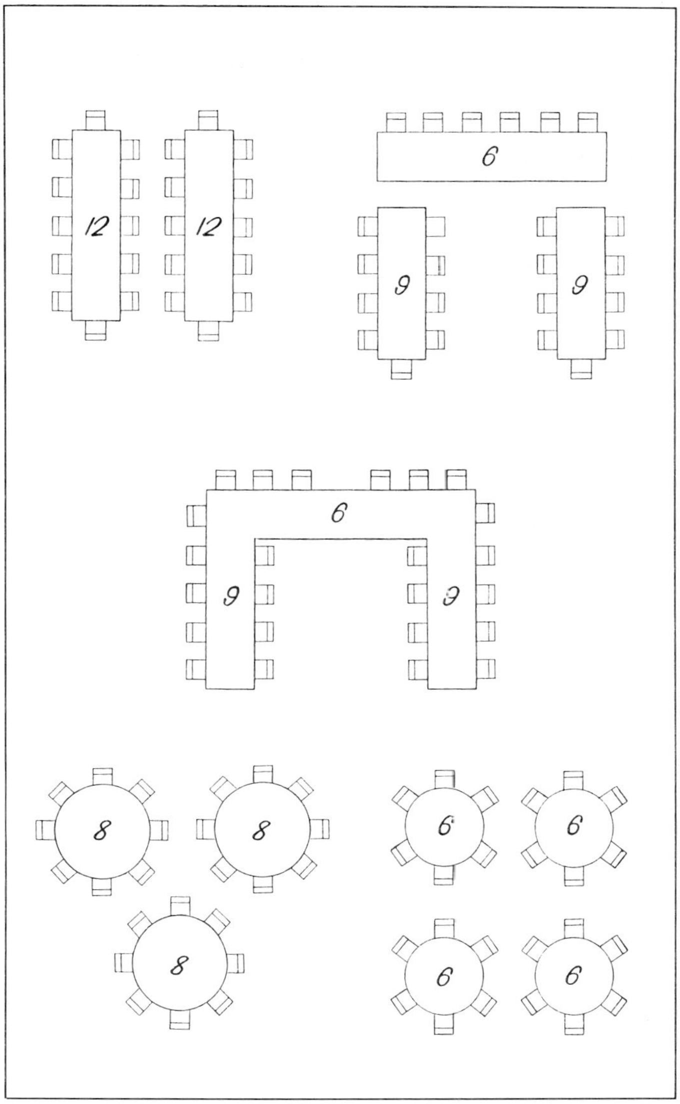

Guidelines for seating 24 persons.

1. If dancing is part of the function, try to determine the number of chairs you'll need on the platform, and other arrangements the band will require.
2. If it's to be strictly a business session, make sure ice water, coffee and ashtrays are provided, along with pencils and writing pads.
3. If the speaker is to use visual aids (and most do in today's visually oriented society), be sure to check this out thoroughly.
4. Find out what equipment he or she will need—movie, overhead or carousel projector, screen, and other items. Who is

Whether it's a community center, civic meeting hall, or lodge, any local facility can be creatively decorated to enhance a party's festive atmosphere.

to provide the equipment, the hotel or the speaker? Perhaps rental will be required. If at all possible, check to see if the equipment is in good operating condition.

5. Round tables take more space than rectangular tables; however, using round tables tends to encourage conversation, if they are not too large.

6. Elevated head tables take considerably more room. Allow 18 inches for each person at the head table, plus 24 inches for the podium. Check steps up to the platform.

While you're at it, check light switches to make certain they're located conveniently. When using a carousel or movie projector, lights must be dimmed for maximum effect. Valuable time can be lost—and continuity disrupted—if the speaker can't quickly and readily control the lighting; or have it controlled by an operator.

And it should almost go without saying, you should check with the hotel to make certain there are adequate electrical outlets, extension cords, and lighting provisions. A meeting can be totally destroyed by an untimely equipment breakdown.

How can you prevent such an embarrassment? Unfortunately, there's no sure-fire solution. The best preventive measure I know is to plan thoroughly, then have a qualified technician on hand during the presentation to come to the rescue if needed. Even then, you are simply minimizing the risk, not eliminating it. You may consider renting a portable battery-operated microphone.

Food and Beverages

When it comes time to decide on what to serve, one of my first questions is, "What's the specialty of the house?" This is not because I feel obligated to take the hotel's suggestion. It's simply a matter of using the very best of what the facility has to offer.

The analogy is simply this: Just as you tend to take the headwaiter's suggestion when you dine out, why not seriously consider the hotel planner's suggestions in deciding your meeting menu?

Incidentally, thorough planning is the key to making even a small gathering a success; *for instance when taking 6 or more guests out to dine. it is always better to make reservations and pre-order part or all of the entire meal.*
Appetizers, salad, and dessert can usually be ordered in advance. This tends to preclude the usual "confusion" of ordering and the resultant long waiting periods. Also, preparation can be done under less intense pressures, which results in improved quality.

For seated luncheons or dinners of more than 6, it is generally better to avoid hot first courses. Keeping production in the kitchen simple generally ensures the quality of the main course and that it will be served on time.

One of the biggest mistakes you are apt to make as a neophyte program chairman is to try to impose your tastes, recipes, and expertise on the local hotel party planner, who knows his facility's capabilities—and limitations—better than you do. It is very difficult for chefs to adapt their commercial expertise to home recipes.

Teamwork is the answer. Try to negotiate on a one-on-one basis. Make suggestions. Even ask to have the chef included in your planning for special food occasions.

How can you be sure that the food presentation meets your expectations? Whether using a professional caterer at home or dining at a hotel, it's wise on special occasions to sample the food. This can be done by having one complete plate of food ordered as a sample or by having a rehearsal meal, which includes all courses. You may be charged, but it's worth it. Your expectations are important, and food-service experts will be happy to please you and your guests.

Beverages

Have a clear understanding with the hotel of *what kind* and *how much* beverage is to be served. Generally, you can estimate that each will consume 2 to 3 drinks per hour. In addition, plan to have white wine available. Its popularity is increasing dramatically. Use the following guide to figure out how much liquor will be required:

1. House brands and special call brands (those ordered by name are more expensive), approximately 20 drinks per fifth, or 26 drinks per quart.
2. Wine—approximately 6 drinks per fifth; 12 drinks per magnum; 72 drinks per case.

Champagne or fruit punch is usually priced per gallon (20 cups per gallon), as is coffee and tea (make sure there's decaffeinated tea and coffee available).

Prices overall are adjustable and depend mainly on the extra labor and bartenders involved. One bartender can accommodate about 50-100 guests, depending on the type of party. You might be able to save by furnishing your own beverages, but some establishments don't allow this.

General Pricing Rules

Room rental is usually prorated according to the number of guests served, the length of time service is required, and the amount of food and beverage consumed.

Food prices are based on the menu, amounts used, and services required. You always have various options, so do not hesitate to exercise your prerogatives here. Service charge and taxes are usually extra.

Predicting the "head count" is a perennial problem for most organizations. For this reason, you should *always* answer invitations to accommodate the hostess as well as the hotel. Most establishments require a guaranteed attendance at least 24 hours in advance. You'll want to anticipate any number of factors that can influence attendance, such as time of year, bad weather, and conflicting activities and events. I try to consider all these factors, come up with my best educated guess, then bite the bullet and give the hotel the guarantee. Often they allow for at least 10 percent extra. You pay the guaranteed number.

Labor is a big factor in figuring costs. Extra labor can include: waiters, bartenders, buffet or extra services, valet parking (usually plan 1 parker for every 50 people—2 persons per car, 25 cars), coat checkers, security personnel, and/or equipment operators.

Items such as table decorations, special cloths and candles might be available from the hotel for your use—*if you ask!*

If the hotel does not have any of the following extra equipment on hand, you may have to use a rental service: decorations, entertainment, tables and chairs, sound equipment, china and glassware, table cloths, piano, portable dance floor and tents (heated).

Showing Your Appreciation

I'm sure you praise the people who help you stage a successful party in your home. Unfortunately, food-service workers in commercial establishments are usually "unsung heroes." These people work long, hard hours, with their busiest times coming at nights, on weekends, and holidays. The pressures of the job are intense because of deadlines and customer expectations.

They deal routinely with the crises you and I encounter in our homes only occasionally. But because of their high level of professionalism, your guests are rarely aware of the breakdown and accidents that happen behind the scenes.

Some of the most talented and gifted food-service people, especially chefs, are unfortunately "hidden" in the kitchen where they rarely get compliments from guests.

I always try to pass on my gratitude to food-service people verbally and in a thank-you note. This will mean a great deal to them, and incidentally, just about ensure your getting the very finest service the next time you use that facility.

Checklist for Planning a Function at a Commercial Establishment

1. Number of guests
2. Arrival time
3. Reception period
4. Meal
5. Program
6. Approximate ending (may be extra charge for exceeding closing time)
7. Furniture arrangement
8. Seating
9. Food service
10. Bar service
11. Dancing (number of chairs on platform for band and other requirements)

12. Meeting—theater style or conference style (pencils, pads, ice water, coffee, ashtrays)
13. Head table—elevated
14. Microphone—standing or on podium (lighted), public-address system
15. Projector, screen, extension cord
16. Piano
17. Flag
18. Platforms—runway (covered, color)
19. Lighting (drapes—open, partial, closed; candles—not at eye level; spotlights)
20. Linens—napkins (colors available, drapes for buffet, head tables, ticket tables. Tables are available that do not require tablecloths. You must know table sizes if you are having cloths other than those provided.)
21. Menu
22. Beverage service

Pay envelope—
for waiters, kitchen help
FLOOR PLAN
rinated Shrimp
lbs. shrimp
cups oil
gallons dry white wine
4 gallons white vinegar
med. purple onions
very finely chopped
tablespoons celery seed
sauce to flavor
Mr. and Mrs.
3016 West
Fort Wor

Chapter Three

Drawing Up Your Party "Game Plan"

Tom Landry tells me he comes up with a carefully thought-out game plan for every Dallas Cowboy football game. Basically, the plan aims to cash in on his own team's strengths and exploit the opposition's weaknesses.

Similarly, I come up with a game plan for *every* party I give. The plan evolves around the things my Party Book tells me I do well. The "opposition" I'm trying to defeat is the crises that can result from poor planning. My four-step party game plan works like this:

Phase I—The Beginning. Decide on the time, date, place, and theme of the party. Make out a guest list and a plan, and send invitations. Confirm caterer and other services.

Phase II—You're On Your Way. Complete and diagram floor plan. Determine what you will need in the way of equipment, furniture, and miscellaneous items. Prepare a menu, and carefully evaluate your food and beverage requirements.

Phase III—The Specifics. Make your purchase lists for all food, beverages, and decorations. Plan extra help, if it's needed. Make a things-to-do list for each day of the week prior to the party date. Make an assignment chart, by name, on your floor plan, showing who is to be where for what.

Phase IV—"The Day." Go over your party plan in its entirety. See checklist for final touches. Prepare pay envelopes. Smile and watch your game plan in action. Best of all, *enjoy your own party!*

The parties I use here are copies from my personal Party Book. I selected them mainly because they represent the different type parties you might be interested in giving at one time or another. For the first party, I spelled out every step I used in applying our party principles and arranged them into four phases. This should give you a good idea of how to follow the format. For the other parties illustrated, only party highlights are given, not every detail.

Some of these parties were rather expensive to stage; some entailed minimal cost. The point is, *you* can control this factor to a great degree. You can make the party extravagantly expensive by hiring caterers, florists, and other professionals; or, you can cut costs dramatically by doing many of the things yourself or by enlisting friends or family and by being *creative and resourceful.*

Major costs are typically labor, food, decorations, and entertainment. By keeping costs down in these areas, you can distinguish yourself as a gracious host or hostess at minimum cost. Keep this point in mind as you go through the planning stages of some of my successes, which included:

1. Brunch After Invitational Golf Tournament
2. Basket Party
3. Texas Barbeque for Eastern Bank Executives
4. Party for the Governor
5. Reception for the Count and Countess
6. Southwest House Party
7. Dinner With Eddie Chiles

8. Take-Me-Out-to-the-Ball-Game Party
9. Family Christmas Party
10. Wedding Reception
11. Accommodating Overnight Guests

The Four-Step Party "Game Plan"

Phase I—The Beginning

Activities		Considerations
Decide	Theme Date Time Location Guest list	Allow for at least 20% regrets.
Confirm	Caterers Services	
Order (or make)	Invitations	Stamps, addresses, and phone numbers.
Send	Invitations	Keep guest list in notebook to check off RSVP.

Phase II—You're on Your Way

Activities		Considerations
Plan	Menu (hors d'oeuvres, main fare, beverages)	Consider what you already have and then determine your menu and what you need. Use your own resources first. The menu determines everything: equipment, furniture, room arrangement, dishes and silverware, place settings, buffet or seated, shopping list, and linens.
Draw	Floor plan	Include food tables, beverage tables, music arrangements, name-tag table, and, if meeting, table and all facilities for speaker and/or program

Phase III—The Specifics

Activities		Considerations
Make list for	Menu	Take all recipes, consider what you have.
	Beverages	Check inventory and make beverage checklist (see Chapter 6).
	Special touches	Candles, flowers or centerpiece, name tags, place cards, and other special rentals.
Plan extra help	Caterers, car parkers, traffic directors, waiters, bartenders, greeters, kitchen help, friends and family to help with flow of party.	Always be specific on: Time needed, expected length of time, pay, dress or uniform, duties.

Activities		**Considerations**
Make list of functions and daily activities for each day of the week prior to the party date; for example	Pick up items on specialty list. Check on furniture. Polish silver. Get out equipment. Set up buffet. Set up bar. Be home for special deliveries and rentals.	Always do as much as possible ahead of party day. Start a week before.
Make assignment chart of your floor plan.	Designate specific areas and duties for helpers, be specific.	
	Caterers	Prepare and serve food.
	Car parkers and traffic director	Park cars or direct traffic. Help people out of cars. Always provide a lane for emergency exit.
	Greeters	Open drapes, light lamps and candles, music, name tags, (pencils, pads, if meeting),hangers for coats; wastebaskets, help watch for burns on carpet or furniture. After party, put out lights, candles, restore area to "clean."
	Waiters	Clean ash trays, watch for burns on carpet and furniture, pick up soiled glasses, serve guests.
	Kitchen help	Prepare hors d'oeuvres 30 minutes before guests arrive. Serve food. Replenish food. Restore kitchen area to "clean." Put away china and silver. Dispose of trash properly.
	Bartender	Set up bar. Replenish drinks and bar wine. Before leaving: Properly cap all bottles. Clean bar area and dispose of trash.
	Babysitter	If necessary.
	With all help, be sure they understand clean-up detail.	Check restrooms. Thoroughly clean assigned areas, rental items. Restore your home or party facilities to normal.

Phase IV—"The Day"

Activities		**Considerations**
You	Go over last-minute checklist. Be flexible. Be calm. Be ready 30 minutes before guests arrive. Be your gracious self. Remember, *people* are more important than protocol, rules, and plans.	Have pay envelopes ready.

Brunch After Invitational Golf Tournament

The "Last-Shot Brunch" was a farewell party for participants in the annual Shady Oaks Invitational Golf Tournament in Fort Worth, Texas. Impulsively, we decided on a Thursday, the opening day of the tournament, to stage the party the following Sunday. Obviously, preparations had to be made on short notice. In addition, we had to prepare the invitations while entertaining house guests Donna and Bud Wilkinson and Reta and Bill Haynes.

Invitations were handed out in the men's locker room. The guest list was quite long and included: Ruth and Bruce Rappaport, Valerie and Ben Hogan, Ann and Bill Mitch, Nancy Lee and Perry Bass, and Adelaide and Bill Fuller.

The "crisis" at this party came quite early—while I was getting ready for the event and, in fact, still had curlers in my hair and a dust mop in my hand. Our home is located near the golf course. When rain interrupted play, several of the invitees—including Dick Moncrief and actor James Garner—rang our doorbell. We were more than happy to offer them refuge.

Even if you aren't ready and have curlers in your hair, you can graciously entertain James Garner, any time!

Brunch After Invitational Golf Tournament

Phase I—The Beginning

Activities			Considerations
Decide	Theme:	Farewell brunch for out-of-town participants in tournament.	
	Date:	Sunday, June 3, 1980	
	Time:	10 a.m.	
	Location:	Host's and hostess's residence	
	Guest list:	Participants in tournament, 120 persons	
Confirm	Caterers		For quail
	Services		Waiters, bartenders, kitchen help Rent: 12 (60-inch round) tables, 120 chairs

Activities		Considerations
Order	Invitations, 75 printed 8½ × 11-inches, to read: *Last-Shot Brunch* Sunday, June 3rd 10 a.m. until 1 p.m. One Western Place Fran and Eddie Chiles RSVP Sue Hill 679-9823	Purchased and printed
Send	Invitations	These were simply handed out in the men's locker room at the tournament.

Phase II—You're on Your Way

Activities		Considerations
Plan	Menu:	
	Candies and nuts	Living room
	Drinks as guests arrive: Champagne	
	White wine Orange blossoms (juice) Screwdrivers Bloody Marys Bull shots	Served from bar

Floor plan for the "Last-Shot" Brunch.

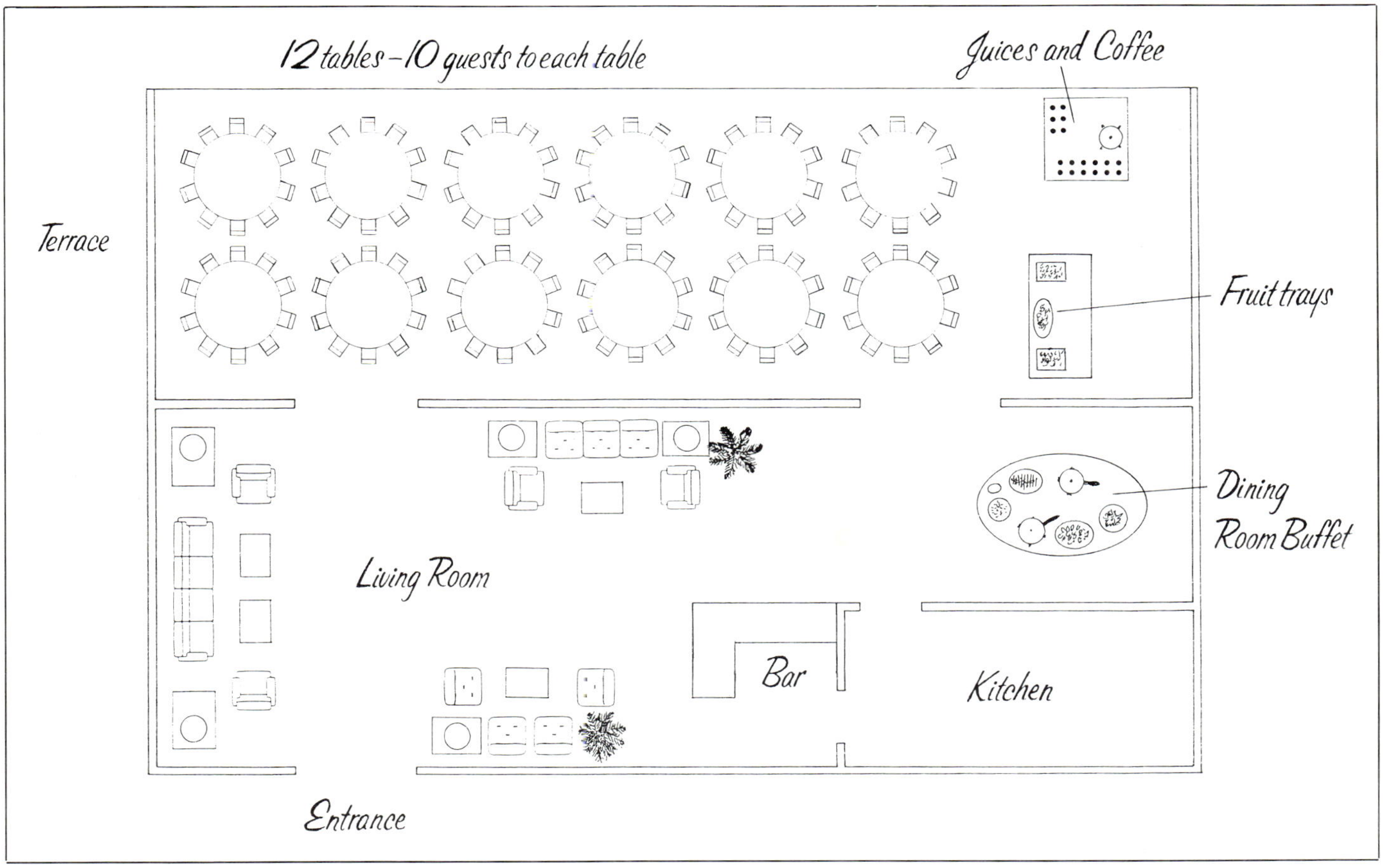

Activities		Considerations
	Tomato, orange juice, coffee	Set on separate table on porch; guests help themselves.
	Main fare—buffet	
	China platters of assorted dried fruits, (figs, apricots, pineapple, and dates)	Buffet—dining room
	Silver trays of fresh pineapple and strawberries, Chinese gooseberries, cherries, papaya, mangoes.	On separate table on porch.
	Chrysanthemum salad in crystal bowl	
	Lemon sugar dressing—Silver tureen (see recipe in Chapter 4)	Buffet—dining room
	Fresh smoked salmon—cream cheese, capers	
	Quail (split lengthwise)	Catered buffet—dining room
	Cream gravy	
	Cheese grits	
	Hot biscuits	
	Coffee	
	Pralines and Millionaires	
Make errand list	*Wednesday (party on Sunday)*	
	Get golf tees and balls at pro shop	
	1 bucket sand	
	Rental Items:	Delivered by rental service and set up.
	35-cup coffee urn	
	30 dinner plates (supplemental)	
	30 dinner forks	
	12 (60-inch) tables	
	90 white and gold folding chairs	
	120 napkins—yellow	
	Purchase:	
	6 dozen tulip champagne glasses	
	Astro-turf (carpet company)	
	Thursday	
	Biscuits	For house guests' breakfast.
	Fresh orange juice	
	Milk	
	Coffee cream	
	Parsley	
	Put salmon in refrigerator	
	Set up buffet—check all equipment	
	Friday	
	Wash and hull strawberries	
	Wash cherries	
	Peel and cut cantaloupe	
	Put plates out for buffet	
	Wash chrysanthemums	
	Make dressing	
	Pick up flowers for arrangements, salad and food garnishes.	
	Fold napkins (get silverware out)	

Activities		Considerations
	Pick up doll (golfer) Check ashtrays	For table centerpiece
	Saturday Wash fruit Butter biscuits	
	Sunday Place cloths on tables. Cut honeysuckle for centerpieces. Prepare centerpieces, place sand in traps. Set up places, food, and put on "final touches."	

Phase III—The Specifics

Activities		Considerations
Make purchase list for	Bar: 4 bottles Bloody Mary mix 1 case bull shot 2 cases champagne 2 cases 7-Up 3 cases cola 1 case club soda 1 case beer 6 dozen tulip champagne glasses (good all-purpose glass for future use.)	This was based on what we already had. Double-check the bar list. Include extra mixes for future use, therefore, buy cases.
	Food: Fruit—fresh 4 flats (12 pints) strawberries 2 lugs cherries with stems 1 flat gooseberries 3 cases mangoes (approx. 9 per case) 3 cases papayas (approx. 6 per case) 30 chrysanthemum blooms 30 cantaloupes 6 lemons, 6 limes 2 lbs cream cheese (salmon) 5 lbs butter 15-lb box pralines (approx. 150) 10-lb box Millionaires Fruit—dried 5 lbs apricots 5 lbs figs 5 lbs dates—pitted 5 lbs pineapple	Order extra for later use. (Picked up at local fruit market, but ordered on Thursday.)
	Special touches: Welcome sign Name tags Flowers	Golf green on table with tees and golf balls—yellow flowers and golfer. (The entire cost for the centerpieces and flowers was minimal.)
Plan extra help	4 car parkers 1 doorman (greeter)	Personnel scheduled from 9 a.m. to 2 p.m.

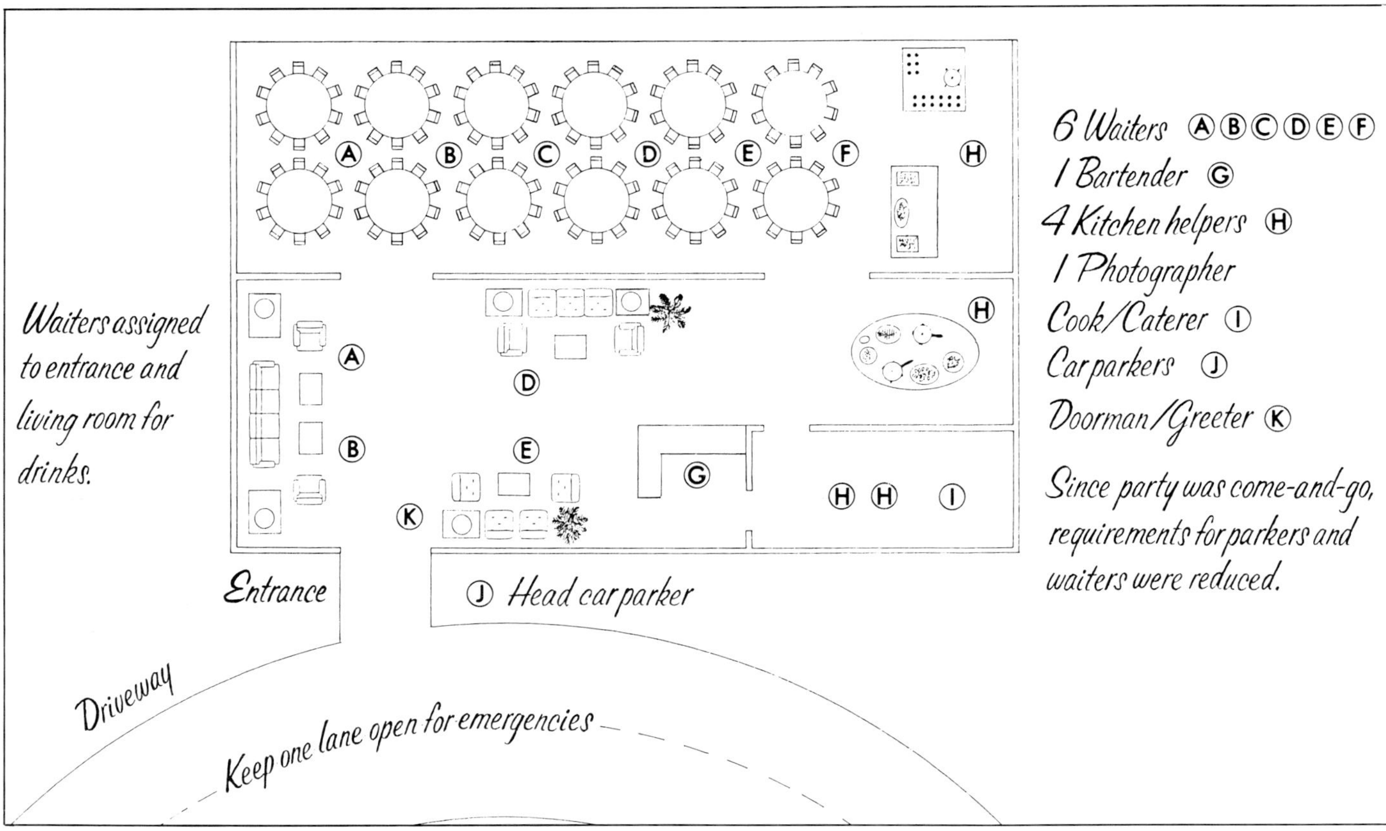

You can avoid a lot of confusion by preparing a floor plan that shows "who will be doing what when."

Activities		Considerations	
	6 waiters		white jackets
	1 bartender	Parkers	black pants
	4 kitchen help (refill buffet		bow ties
	and dishes) preparation	Doorman	
	1 photographer	Waiters	tuxedos
	Caterer supplies cook and	Bartenders	
	fryer for quail and biscuits	Kitchen—	white blouses/shirts
			black skirts/pants

Phase IV—"The Day"

Activities		Considerations
You	Go over checklist.	Have pay envelopes ready.
	Get dressed and ready.	
	Put fresh flowers on fruit trays.	
	Ice champagne and white wine.	
	1 silver tray—tomato juice.	
	1 silver tray—orange juice.	
	Set up silver for serving.	
	Do fruit trays.	
	Garnish salmon.	
	Double check men's and women's restrooms.	
	Other food—quail.	
	Chrysanthemum salad.	After clean up—happy ending and pay time.

Basket Party

Here's an all-purpose party that can be given for just about any occasion. The basket party is easy to plan and give. And it's inexpensive. You can do the entire production yourself—from preparation to serving.

Everything can be planned in advance, and serving and clean-up efforts are minimized.

The party can be held indoors or outdoors; by the pool or on the patio; or on a picnic. It can be adapted to just about any occasion or age group.

Helium-filled balloons tied to the baskets make the party more festive for adults as well as children. However, one or two balloons to a basket is enough. You don't want your party to fly too high!

You can also use a watermelon or any self-contained object for your party in place of an actual basket. (See watermelon basket recipe in following section.)

If you don't have baskets, use boxes. One way is to cover brown boxes with pretty wrapping paper, and to decorate with art work or appropriate stickers. You can simplify the menu by eliminating the cantaloupe basket and merely putting food on the plate. The individual boxes are a good idea for "tail-gate" parties at football games. Pack picnic style food that is easy to eat, so you can just open the tail-gate and serve, before or after your favorite game.

The basket party inspires and encourages good communication among your guests. It's great fun and *always* a success! This party was for a bride. The basket was made for 2 guests each, with tables set up for a minimum place setting.

Basket Luncheon

Phase I—The Beginning

Activities			Considerations
Decide	Theme:	Bridal luncheon	
	Date:	Tuesday, June 2	
	Time:	12 noon	
	Location:	Residence	
	Guest list:	Supplied by bride—30 people (plus a few personal friends).	
Confirm	Caterers.		Two girls for final service and clean-up on day of party (we prepared all the food).
Order	Hand-made invitations		

Activities		Considerations
Send	Invitations	
	Highlights and Ideas	
	Menu:	
	As guests gather—	
	Cranberry frost	
	White wine	
	12:30—	
	Chicken salad topped with toasted coconut chips in cantaloupe with fresh flower on each, garnished with fruit and fresh mint.	All put in basket to serve 2 guests each.
	Two cheeses (waffle sliced)—cheddar and mozzarella	Each basket is served on table between each 2 guests.
	Graber olives	
	Rice crackers	
	Iced tea with orange wedge	
	Dessert:	
	Passed basket of whole fresh peaches and/or individually wrapped pralines (these can be included inside lunch baskets).	No extra plates needed.
	We set up tables with placemats, 1 fork, napkin and plate. A personal friend hosted each table informing guests to take cantaloupe from basket and place on plate to eat.	Gardenias or daisies work nicely as flower on cantaloupe. Balloons can be tied to the basket handles, personalized by writing welcome or a greeting and the guests' names.

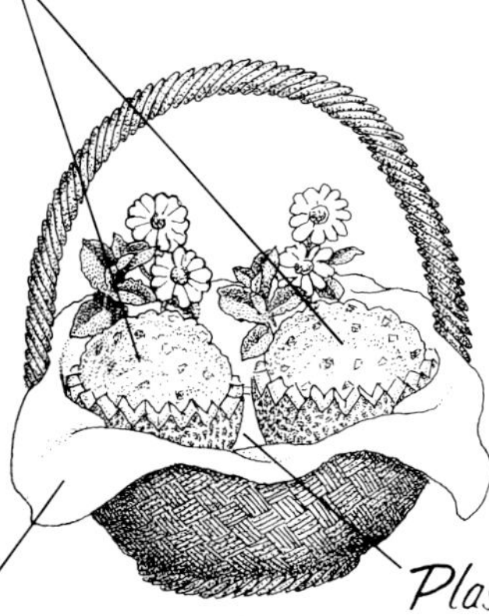

Watermelon Basket
Serves 4

1 sugar baby watermelon (approximately 14 inches long)
4 servings chicken salad
4 servings mixed fresh fruit
1 healthy sprig of mint
Pretty flowers (daisies, carnations, zinnias, etc., from your yard.)
Small flag with message (Bon Voyage, Welcome Mary, Happy Birthday, etc.)

Make preparations the day before your party. Assemble the morning of the party. Select watermelons approximately 12 to 14 inches long so they will fit your dinner plate or platter. Trim each end approximately 1 inch.

Cut watermelon lengthwise into fourths. Slice each section across the bottom so it will sit on the plate.

With an ice cream scoop, hollow a hole at each end of the watermelon. Save meat and dice in small pieces for fruit salad. Place chicken salad in one hole and fruit salad in the other.

Chicken Salad for Watermelon Basket

Make your favorite chicken salad the day before your party. Remember to use bite-size or small diced pieces of chicken so it will fit in the melon, and avoid using the same fruit in the chicken salad as you plan to use in the fruit salad, such as green grapes. Put the chicken salad in the hole in the melon. Garnish with

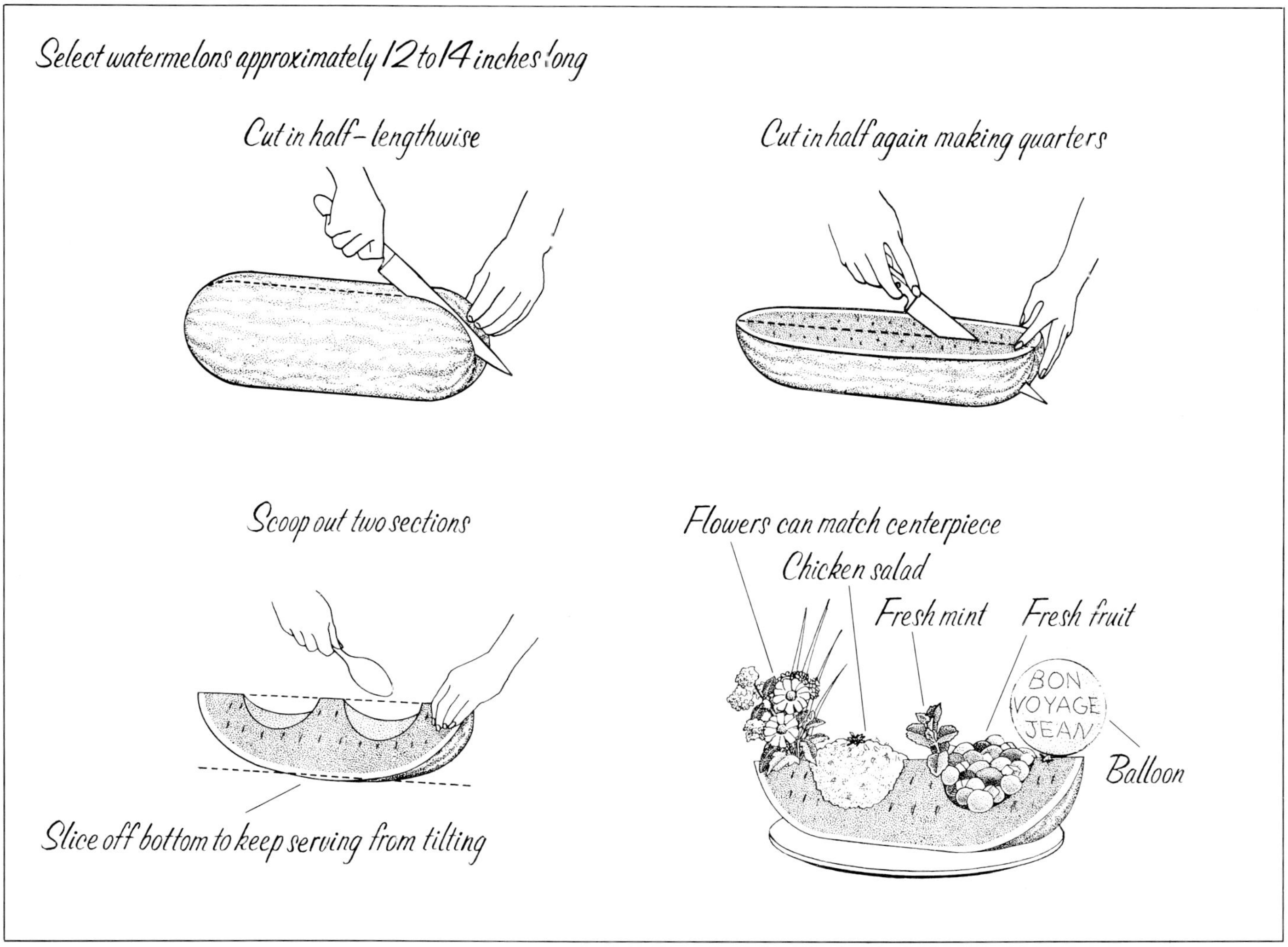

slivered nuts or toasted coconut chips. Fresh flowers may be placed at each end of the basket, or a flower at one end and a small flag message at the other.

Fruit Salad for Watermelon Basket

Combine papaya, melon balls, pineapple tidbits, seedless grapes, diced apples in bowl and let chill overnight in pineapple juice. Clean strawberries, blueberries, kiwi, dark cherries. On the day of your party, drain the fruit and place it in the holes of the watermelon. Top with blueberries, cherries, kiwi, fresh strawberries, and mandarin oranges.

Top with bouquet of mint in melon beside fruit.

You may use small balloons and write a message on each. Place a toothpick under a rubber band tied to the balloon, and stick in the end of the melon.

Melons can be completed the morning of party and placed in the refrigerator. Put them on plates on the table before guests are seated. Just provide a fork and napkin.

These are so pretty on your table that your centerpiece can be very simple. You may use the same flowers to match the ones on the melons. This is one of my favorites and a creation I did years ago at The Houston Club.

Texas Barbecue for Eastern Bank Executives

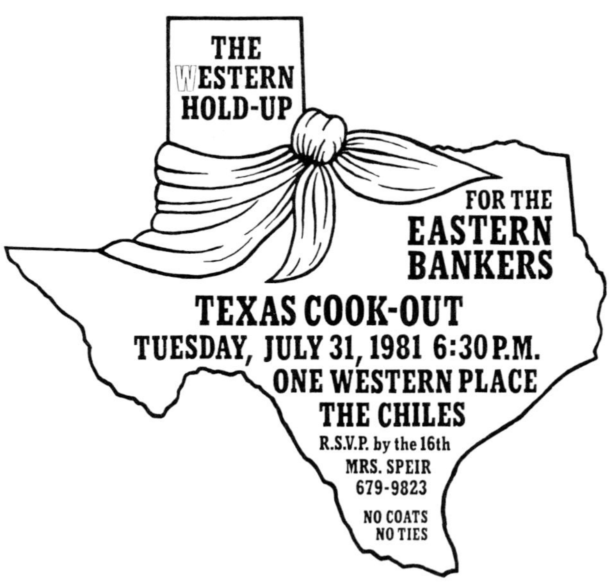

This party was given in honor of John McGillicuddy, chairman of the board of Manufacturers Hanover Trust Company of New York, and his associates, Conrad Albert and John Sullivan.

What does one serve New York banking executives? Admittedly, a number of exotic dishes were considered. But in the final analysis, we opted for what we do best—a good, old-fashioned Texas-style barbecue. Remember, it's part of my philosophy to serve food that's a specialty of your own area when entertaining out-of-towners.

A special touch for the bankers was the added attraction on the centerpieces. We placed stick-on coins (which looked genuine!) on the ribbons and had our honorees' names inscribed thereon. We also had a big "Welcome John" sign on our front door.

Upon leaving, the guests were presented specially prepared favors for their wives: Conna McGillicuddy, Betsy Albert, and Madeline Sullivan. The favors were engraved, silver-bullet key chains.

Place cards were clear plastic boxes that held sand, a small oil derrick, and a flag with guests' names.

A major crisis at this party took place when a guest who had declined days before, came at the last minute. Naturally, there was no engraved key chain for his wife, but we substituted a plain one and added a place at the table. And we were quick about it!

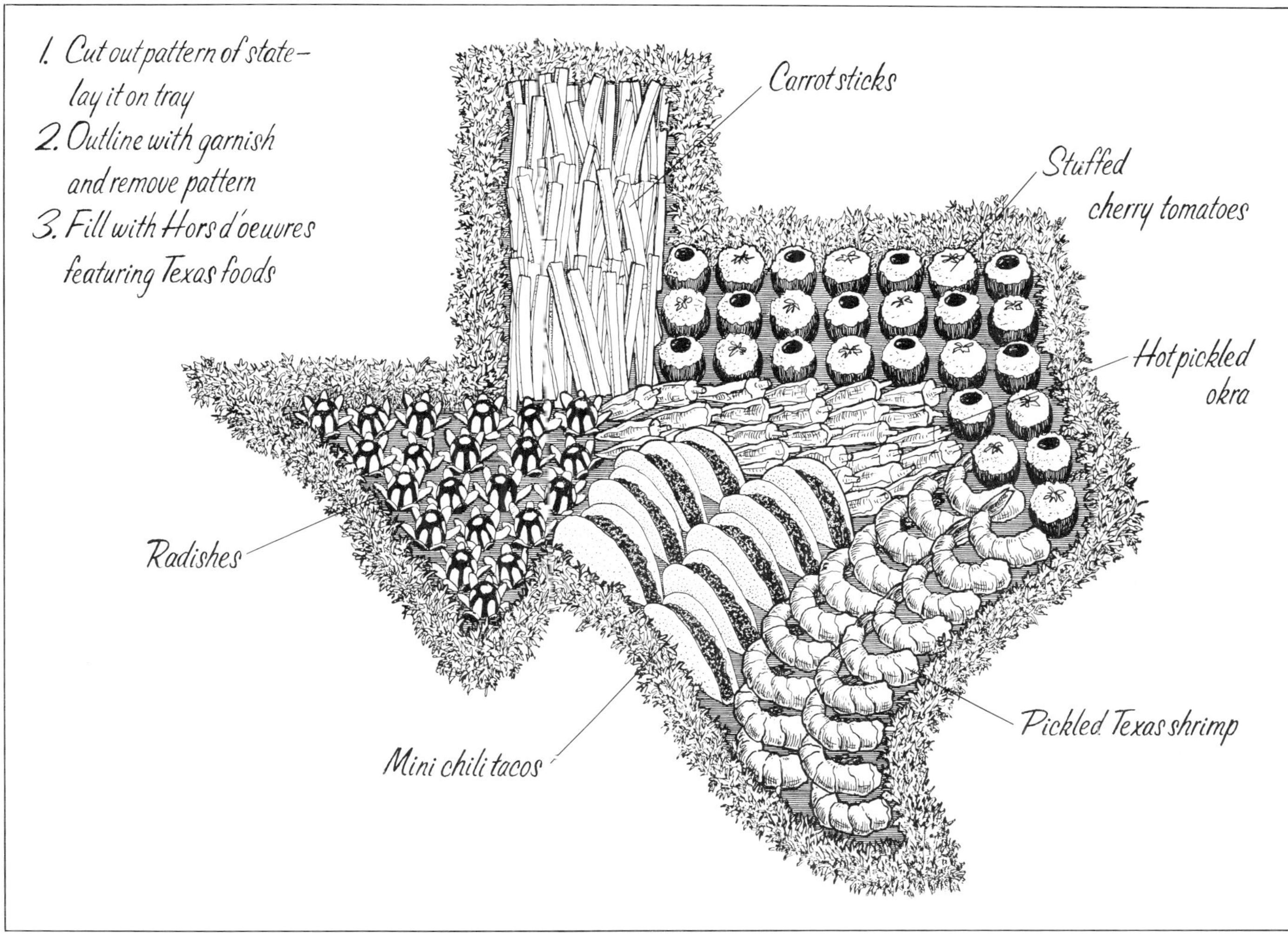

This Lone Star State centerpiece was a big hit with the Eastern bankers.

Texas Barbecue for Eastern Bank Executives

Phase I—The Beginning

Activities		**Considerations**
Decide	Theme: Texas Barbecue Time: 6:30 p.m. Location: Residence Guest list: 18 people	
Confirm	Invitations—printed and mailed.	Chairs Rent tables—one 72-inch round table; two 6-foot rectangles
	Barbecue cook Bartender 3 Waiters 2 Kitchen helpers	Steak knives

Activities	Highlights and Ideas	Considerations
	Menu:	
	Special Texas hors d'oeuvre tray	
	Buffet: served at table by waiters.	
	Caesar salad	
	Texas-size sirloin strips	Special cut 1½-inch thick, 12 to 14 ounces each.
	Ranch style beans (prepared in Fort Worth)	
	Crescent rolls	Six bottles of 1964 Chateau Mouton Rothschild
	Fresh fruit dessert—papaya half filled with fresh melon and berries	
	Cappuccino (see Chapter 6 for recipe)	
Draw outside floor plan. Seat 6 people at each table. Arrange tables to keep everyone together to give equal opportunity to be near special guest.		Welcome sign on entrance Candy and nuts Fresh flowers Hors d'oeuvre tray Bar—waiter serves drinks from bar inside by order Yellow fingertip towels are used for napkins

Party for the Governor

Time is of the essence in staging certain parties. And so it was for a party we gave for former Texas Governor Bill Clements and his first lady, Rita. Other guests were Jane and John Justin, Janice and Dee Kelly, George Ann and Amon Carter, Eulema and George Brown, and Jerri and Billy Bob Watt.

You might say the party shaped up pretty much like a typical political event. The Governor, first lady, and guests had only an hour-and-a-half to socialize, eat dinner, and arrive at the Fort Worth Fat Stock Show on time for opening night at the rodeo.

Our theme was Texas-Western. It featured Lone Star State native wine; oil-derrick and armadillo candles; yucca and cactus centerpieces arranged in granite frying pans; and leather, Texas-shaped place cards mounted on tiny barbed-wire fences.

As usual, there was a crisis—the number of guests changed. The Governor unexpectedly brought an aide. We simply added a place setting (ignoring the place card) and got the show on the road. Everyone had a great time.

Rule:

The most important female guest is seated to the host's right. The most important male guest is seated to the right of the hostess.

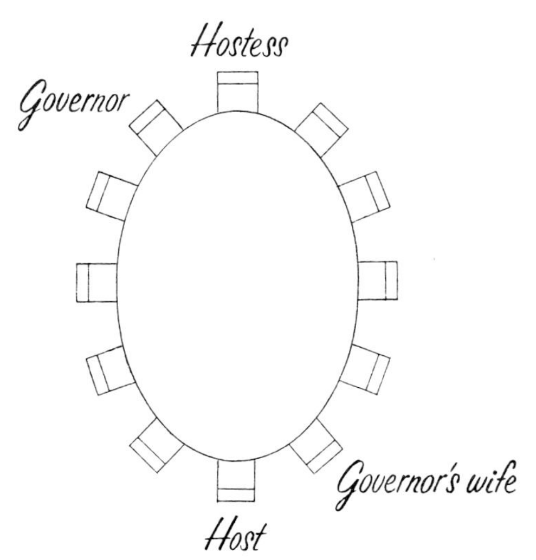

Governor's Party

Phase I—The Beginning

Activities	Considerations
Decide	Theme: Texas Date: January 25th Time: 6:30 p.m.—guests had to leave for rodeo at 7:45 p.m. Location: Residence Guest list: 12 people
Confirm	Caterers Flowers and decor
Invitations	By telephone

Highlights and Ideas

Menu:

Apple with Seafood First Lady (see recipe in Chapter 5)

Tournadoes Governor—twin filets of beef (one with fresh mushroom cap, one with hollandaise sauce and truffle)

Individual acorn squash with spinach souffle

Shoestring carrots

Texas wine

Petite buttered rolls

Cranberry sherbet with blueberries in cotton candy (Form cotton candy into nest. Fill with scoop of sherbet—top with fresh blueberries and a Texas flag. See recipe in Chapter 4.)

Special Touches:

Flower arrangements were made of cactus, yucca, and yellow mums in granite-ware frying pans.

We used armadillo and oil-derrick candles with branding irons lying on the table.

The place cards were made of a 4-inch piece of leather in the shape of the state of Texas, on which the guests' names were stamped. The leather states were mounted on miniature barbed wire fences and surrounded with artificial bluebonnets—the state flower.

Reception for the Count and Countess

Eddie and I ran into our friends, the Count and Countess de Romanones of Spain (Aline and Luis) at a Young Presidents' Organization meeting in Austin. We invited them for room and board if they found themselves near Fort Worth. Sure enough, they took us up on our offer sooner than expected. Aline agreed to speak to our guests on "Keeping America Free." They were to arrive on, of all days, Halloween.

Aline is a fascinating lady. A native New Yorker, she met and married the Count while living in Madrid. They were in the process of "living happily ever after" when Spain's political climate turned a bit "stormy."

This caused Aline to become very concerned about the freedom in our beloved America. Since that time, she has been touring the United States, warning our citizenry to become involved and heed Solzhenitsyn's advice that Americans can keep their freedoms only if they get involved in our political system at the grass-roots level. It's never going to start in Washington!

After the Count and Countess arrived, we had exactly a day and a half to get ready for the party, invite everyone, and have the food and beverage ready for the reception in their honor.

The situation obviously called for some quick decision-making. I called about 10 close friends—including some relatives—and got each to agree to call about 15 people. For such short notice, we came up with a sizeable crowd.

Emphasis was placed on simple elegance in planning the food and centerpiece for the hors d'oeuvre table.

The "guests" we didn't expect turned out to be young Halloween trick-or-treaters. They seemed to arrive just as we were receiving the guests and introducing the Count and Countess. Indeed, it turned out to be fun handing out treats to the young goblins with one hand and receiving our more sophisticated guests with the other.

Reception for the Count and Countess de Romanones

Phase I—The Beginning

Activities		Considerations
Decide	Theme: Reception Date: October 31, 1981 Time: 7:30 p.m. Place: Residence Guest list: To have as many guests as possible we invited specific friends by phone and asked them to invite their friends.	The Count and Countess arrived on short notice. They were here only one night. We wanted as many people as possible to hear the Countess's speech concerning "Keeping America Free."
Confirm	Services—flowers, traffic director, kitchen help, waiters, helper for coats, and provide name tags for each guest to write his or her own.	

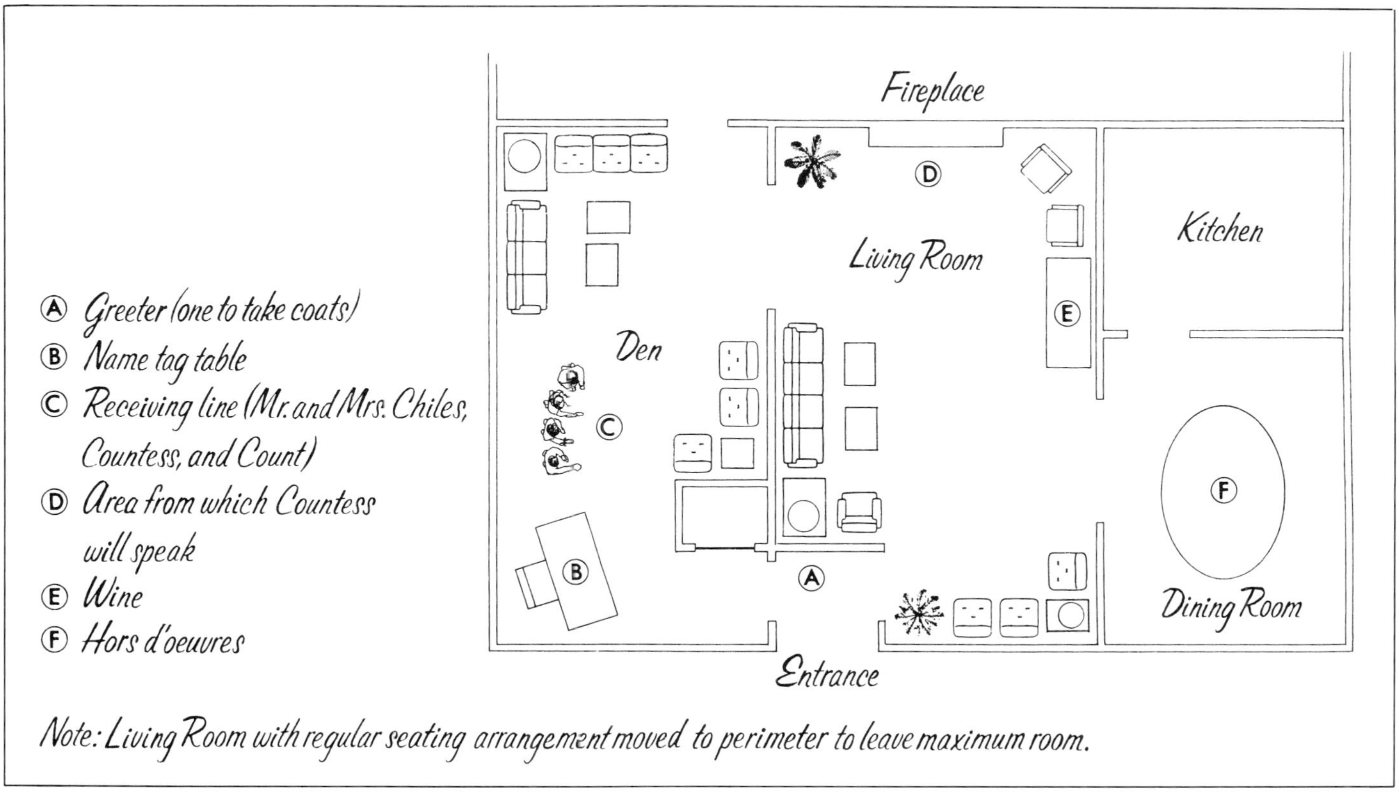

Putting hors d'oeuvres farther from the entrance assured a smooth flow of guests through the den and living room.

Phase II—You're on Your Way

Activities		Considerations
Plan	Menu: Hors d'oeuvre table for reception Salmon and caviar fish spread (see Chapter 5) Fran's Hors d'oeuvres (see Recipes and Special Tips in Chapter 5) Paté Orange-nut bread, party rye Ham, Jarlsberg cheese Dried fruit (apricots, figs, peaches, dates) Cookies, macaroons, apricot squares, chocolate divinity	
	Beverages White wine Champagne	I decided not to serve mixed drinks. Guests were coming to meet the Count and Countess and to hear the Countess's message. This was an effort to keep it simple and sober.

Southwest House Party

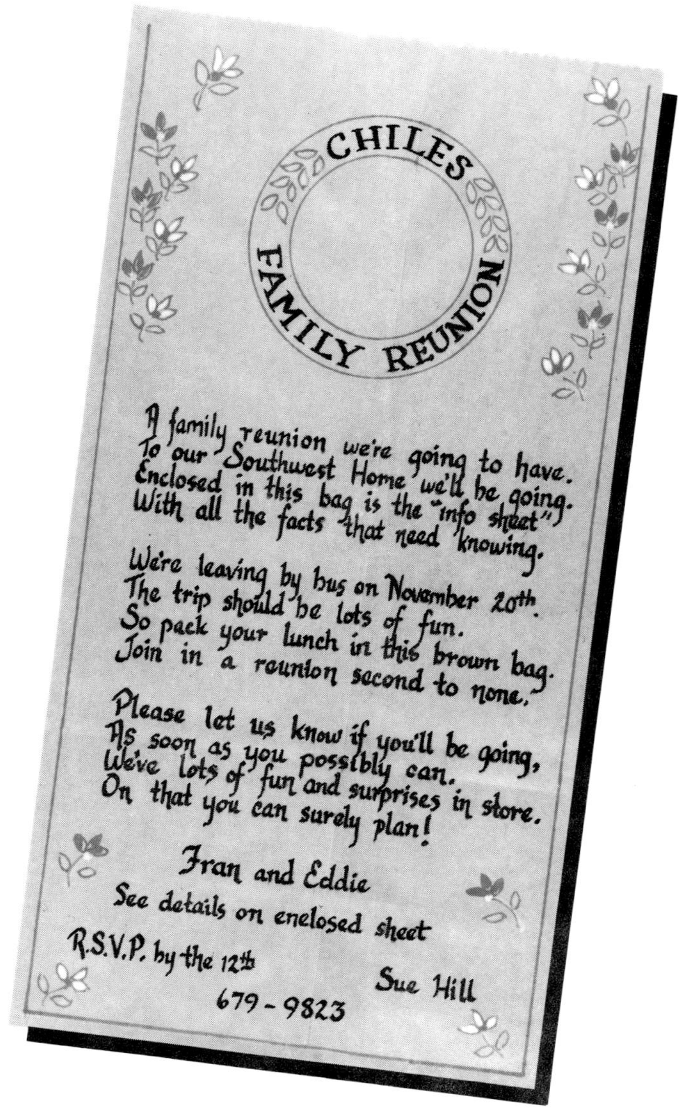

This party was "all in the family." You probably know what I'm talking about—the proverbial family reunion.

Again in this case, good planning paid off. I know it sounds repetitious, but I'm still constantly amazed—and quite pleased—by how solid planning tends to reduce frictions and conflicts, and contributes to everyone's pleasure. Particularly important, wouldn't you say, for a *family* affair?

For all practical purposes, we did this one without helpers, except for one lady who worked extra during the day as housekeeper. And I might add parenthetically that even if you do have help these days, you normally don't have their services on weekends and evenings.

We solved the problem, in this case, by dividing the duties among specific guests and members of the family. Too, we had an open-door policy. As guests arrived, we took them on a tour of the kitchen and told them to ring for service if they liked. But we also assured them that nothing would happen!

Our solution was to make everyone feel at home, and when hungry or thirsty to help themselves. If their beds got turned down at night, it was because Eddie and I slipped into the guest rooms and performed the magic act ourselves.

Our self-styled "helpers" performed marvelously.

Southwest House Party

Phase I—The Beginning

Activities	Considerations
Decide	Theme: Family Reunion Date: November 20, 1980 Time: Thursday through Sunday Location: Southwest Home
Confirm.................	No caterers Housekeeper in home
Order..................	Invitations handmade and mailed with general plans of schedule

Activities	Considerations
	enclosed. Mailed about 2 months in advance of party.
Send.	Information sheets of complete schedule for weekend mailed to each guest (total of 12) 3 weeks in advance. (See following page.)

Southwest House Party Information Sheet

November 1980
To: All Guests
From: Fran and Eddie
Agenda for Chiles' Reunion
Thursday through Sunday
Your Name ______________________
Complete Address ______________________
Telephone Number ______________________

Thursday

1:30 p.m.	Arrive at house, unpack and "settle in."
2:30 p.m.	Go to club for lunch—dress casual.
3:30 p.m.	Return to house.
	Swim—Visit—Explore
7:00 p.m.	Bars set up—self-service—everyone is free to help himself at any time. Coffee, snacks, beverages, etc.
8:00 p.m.	Dinner at home.
	Moonlight, roses, and "nitey nite."
Friday and Saturday	
	Early birds plug in coffee and help yourself.
9:00 a.m.	Breakfast—house
10:00 a.m.–4:00 p.m.	Your choice—golf, tennis at the club, touring, swimming, shopping, cards. Lunch—where you are! Snacks at home.
4:00–6:00 p.m.	Quiet hours—rest or whatever you like.
7:00 p.m.	Cocktails—dress casual, home.
8:00 p.m.	Cook-out by "Chef Host," home.
Note:	Cocktails on Saturday night at home—garden dinner and dancing at hotel, dress up.
Sunday	
9:00 a.m.	Breakfast, relax, and pack.
12:00 p.m.	Light lunch.
1:00 p.m.	Leave for airport on bus. (We had a birthday celebration on the bus to the airport as a surpise for one guest. This included cake, balloons, and champagne.)

Menu Plan for Southwest Weekend

Breakfast	**Lunch**	**Snacks—7:00 p.m.**	**Dinner—8:00 p.m.**
Thursday	Club	Toasted pecans Crab fingers, red sauce Cheese	Smoked turkey Roast beef Cranberry relish Mustard, relish, mayonnaise, Small rolls Green salad with bean sprouts and pomegranate seeds, roquefort, oil & vinegar, pumpernickel and wheat bread iced tea, coffee, wine
Friday Grapefruit or Melon Ham Scrambled eggs Cottage cheese, Danish, toast, jams Coffee	Club or everyone on his own	Miniature avocados with lemon juice Smoked almonds	Steaks à la Chef Eddie Baked beans Tossed salad French bread Coffee Fresh raspberry cheese cake
Saturday Fruit or juice Sausage and bacon Scrambled eggs Coffee cake Coffee	Everyone on his own	Paté Caramel corn with almonds	Dinner—hotel & Dancing
Sunday Fruit Eggs to order Sausage, ham Toast, jam, butter Coffee	Cold cuts Corned beef and peppered beef, rye Cheese, pickles, relish, mustard (self service)		On bus to airport, birthday cake! Champagne

Bowls of fresh fruit daily in living room.
Fresh flower to go on each pillow—Saturday night!

Southwest House Party—Assignments for Housekeeper

The following tasks may be assigned to family members, if you don't have a housekeeper. But whoever helps should be given one week's advance notice of their duties.

Wednesday

Get dishes out for buffet, slice ham for breakfast, wash lettuce. Slice smoked turkey and beef. Double check all bedrooms and bathrooms.

Thursday

When guests go to lunch:

1. Place toasted pecans in dishes in living room.
2. Set up coffee for breakfast.
3. Put fresh fruit in bowl.
4. Set up bar.
5. Set tables for dinner.

6:30 p.m.—Replenish bar, glasses, etc. Set up hors d'oeuvres (crab claws, red sauce, and cheese).
7:00 p.m.—Guests have cocktails

Housekeeper prepares dinner to serve at 8:00 p.m. Serving spoons and forks on each item, buffet style.

8:00 p.m.—Large tray with sliced smoked turkey around dish of cranberry relish; large tray with sliced roast beef around dish with mustard relish.
Garnish with greens and fresh flowers.
Large bowl with mixed green salad with bean sprouts, pomegranate seeds, roquefort, oil and vinegar dressing.
Pumpernickel and whole wheat bread.
Ice water in each glass on table.
Place wine out on bar with wine glasses for self-service.
Make decaffeinated coffee.
Prepare dishes for breakfast.
"Good night."

Friday

8:00 a.m.—Start coffee at 8 a.m. and make breakfast for guests: grapefruit halves, melon wedges on large trays, sweet rolls, buttered toast, jam on buffet, coffee, scrambled eggs with cottage cheese, grilled ham slices.
9:00 a.m.—Guests for breakfast
10:00 a.m.—Clear breakfast tables and clean up.
Make beds, do baths, laundry, check ash trays, water plants, etc.
Check pool area for glasses, ashtrays. Clean lettuce, produce, fruit, and help with dinner items and breakfast preparation. Aid guests with lunch, beverages and requests. Replenish ice at bar.
11:30 to 12:00—Housekeeper gets her lunch and rests during afternoon.
6:00 p.m.—Set up bar and hors d'oeuvres.
7:00 p.m.—Cheese, miniature avocados and crackers (garnish).
Set tables for dinner, ice water, etc.
Make salad, prepare bread, set plates up and aid host.
8:00 p.m.—Charcoal steaks
Baked beans
Tossed salad, oil & vinegar dressing
Hot French bread
Cheese cake with raspberries
Coffee

Saturday

Same schedule until 2:00 p.m. Breakfast: fruit, scrambled eggs, sausage, toast, jam, butter, coffee cake.
2 to 6 p.m.—Rest.
6:00 p.m.—Set up cocktails and hors d'oeuvres
Paté and caramel corn.
7:45 p.m.—Guests to leave to go out for dinner.
Clean up, turn down guests beds and put a flower on each pillow.
Happy Rest!

Sunday

8 a.m. to 3 p.m.—Help with breakfast and lunch.
9:00 a.m.—Breakfast for guests: fruit, eggs, sausage/ham, toast, jam, butter, coffee
12:00—Buffet lunch: sliced thin corn beef, mustard, sliced thin pepper beef, cheese, pickles, relish—guests to make own sandwich
Move most food possible to freezer and put away all beverages.
Help ensure that guests get *everything* packed.
Clean up.

Dinner with Eddie Chiles

It's not every wife who would auction off her husband. But I did it—for art's sake!

The occasion was a fund-raising auction staged by Rita and Harry Moore in Oklahoma City. Highest bidder and guests were to be flown to Fort Worth for dinner and an entertaining evening with Eddie "I'm Mad" Chiles.

The winning couple donated several thousand dollars to the arts for this honor. "It was worth every penny," the happy winners said later.

The crisis at this function happened when the winners arrived at Eddie's home. They were greeted by a local high school band, which understandably did not know the Oklahoma University fight song. So what did they play? *The Eyes of Texas,* until we quickly switched them to the theme from the Olympics. Mercy!

The guests simply smiled and carried on. Before leaving, however, they did promise to mail the local band sheet music for *Boomer Sooners.*

Dinner with Eddie Chiles

Phase I—The Beginning

Activities

Decide	Theme: Dinner With Eddie Chiles Date: March 3, 1981 Time: 7 p.m. Place: Residence
Confirm	14 People

Phase II—You're on Your Way

Activities

Plan	Menu: Individual smoked salmon with cream cheese and caviar (see recipe in Chapter 5) Roast tenderloin—natural juice Wild rice Yellow squash crowns filled with red beet puree Small buttered rolls Bordeaux wine Pineapple volcano (see recipe in Chapter 4) Liqueurs and brandy in living room

Activities	**Considerations**
	Highlights and Ideas *Special Touches:* Two limousines to meet guests at airport. High school band played guests' state song as limousine entered driveway, lights were turned out for full effect and brought up as they arrived. *Gifts:* An engraved cup "Dinner with Fran and Eddie Chiles—(date)" (Individually gift wrapped and given to each guest as they departed.)

A Prize At An Out-of-State Auction

The following poem was in script on parchment paper, tied with a bow, and placed at each place setting:

F or times like these we are so thankful,
R emembering our Lord so kind
A nd the blessings of these friendships
N ew and bringing old friends to mind.

A nd especially this evening we'd like to say,
N othing could please us more;
D ining with you as guests in our home,

E njoying what God has in store.
D enoting our blessings, we give our thanks,
D elighted that you are here.
I n time we hope you will return.
E ach one, God keep you near.

Fran and Eddie

Take-Me-Out-to-the-Ballgame Party—"Eddie's Happy"

In 1977, my husband launched his famed "Eddie's Mad" campaign, in which he spoke out against ever-increasing government spending and growth.

The 60-second radio spots were broadcast regularly in 14 states for 3 years through November 1980. The "Eddie's Mad" theme caught the public's imagination and became a household phrase.

I planned a surprise birthday party for Eddie using a switcheroo—an "Eddie's Happy" theme. All decorations (streamers, balloons, matches) were printed with "Eddie's Happy." The Stadium Club at Ranger Stadium, where we held the party, was decorated from top to bottom with

"Eddie's Happy" signs. In addition, a red, white, and blue color scheme matched the club decor. We even had red table cloths, thanks to the club.

Invitees included Winnie and Joe Humphrey, Opal and Mack Rankin, Wendy and Mac Churchill, Maurine and Joe Lydick, Mary Frances and Bill Conner, Rex Cross, Wylodean and Bill Saxon, Jane and Tom Larimore, Deborah and Tex Moncrief, Margaret and Trammell Crow, Gay and Jim Simmons, Nancy and Norm Brinker, and Lt. General D. A. Thompson. It so happened Governor Clements and his wife, Rita, were to meet us at the ball-park entrance. Naturally, we had to leave for the ball game early to meet them on time.

Needless to say, Eddie was genuinely surprised by the crowd upon his arrival, and was very happy—as he *really* is!

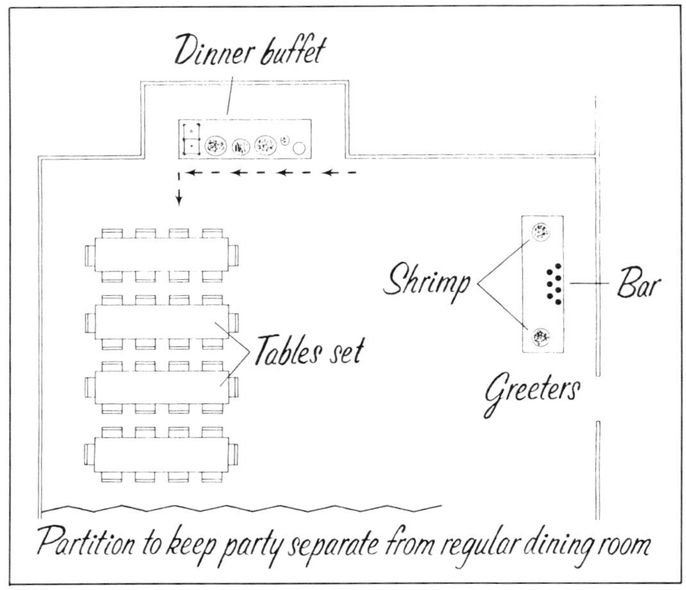

Floor plan of the stadium party

Take Me Out to the Ball Game!

Phase I—The Beginning

Activities		Considerations
Decide	Theme: Surprise happy birthday at Ranger Stadium Club Date: June 6, 1981 Time: 5:45 p.m. Guests arrive 6:00 p.m. Honoree arrives 7:30 p.m. Game time	
	40 people	We arranged to pick up the honoree, thus allowing time for the guests to arrive first for the surprise.
Order	Invitations	Reserved seats were assigned, special parking tickets and seating tickets were distributed beforehand.

Phase II—You're on Your Way

Activities		Considerations
Plan	Menu:	
	Iced shrimp served as guests arrived	Catered by the club restaurant
	6:15 p.m.:	Table settings were set ahead of time.
	Prime rib with horseradish sauce Fresh asparagus	Singing telegrams were delivered—arranged by guests.
	Carrots Au gratin potatoes	Note: Selection of items was limited to expedite service.
	Rolls	Photographer
	Black Forest birthday cake with candles (Eddie's favorite) Champagne	

Activities		Considerations
Make list	Catered food	
	5–10-foot rectangular tables	Rented for buffet and dinner tables, to be used in Club.
	Bows and 550 streamers in red and blue printed with "Eddie's Happy"	
	550 Balloons attached to ceiling with "Eddie's Happy" on each.	Ordered and set up by a party service.
	Streamers on buffet	
	100 balloons in each box	
	Bar and screens in red, white, and blue	
	No-seam ribbons with "Eddie's Happy"	Colors were in keeping with the stadium club decor and Ranger uniforms.
	Helium for balloons	
	200 napkins with "Eddie's Happy"	

"Eddie's Happy" at Ranger Stadium

Family Christmas Party

Christmas parties have become traditional in many families, and ours is no exception.

Our annual party started with 12 people several years ago and at last count stood at 50. It's still growing and, of course, includes friends and "new" relatives as the family grows.

We like to exchange gifts and have entertainment consistent with the true meaning of Christmas. A special Christmas reading or story, religious music or a pageant telling the story of the birth of Jesus Christ adds to the meaning of our gathering. I like to give Christian books or jewelry. These gifts serve as a reminder, all year long, of the family celebration and our Savior.

I planned and served all the food, but it's fun—and economical—to have each guest bring a dish. Plan your meals ahead and assign various members of your family to salads, desserts, meats, and so forth.

Read over my game plan for a family Christmas party and maybe you can use some of these ideas in your own situation.

Family Christmas Party

Phase I—The Beginning

Activities		Considerations
Decide	Theme: Family Christmas Party Date: December 22, 1981 Time: 6:30 p.m. Location: Residence	
	50 people	
	Invitations	Some mailed and others hand-delivered.
Confirm	Caterers plus other personnel.	
	Rental—tables and folding chairs.	60-inch round tables. I used my own tablecloths and chair backs especially made to match color theme in living room. (made to fit rental tables and chairs.) These cloths are used for parties throughout the year.
	Highlights and Ideas	
Plan	Menu: Cranberry Frost—Wine Table	

Activities		Considerations
	Buffet: Roast wild turkey/giblet gravy Smoked Turkey Baked ham/mustard sauce Cornbread dressing Individual acorn squash with spinach souffle. grated Swiss cheese on top and pomegranate seeds Apple, walnut, julienne beets, endive, Bibb lettuce and watercress salad, classical French dressing Pumpkin bread and small buttered croissants Decaffeinated coffee Christmas ice cream ring flambé (see recipe in Chapter 4)	Used two wild turkeys we had been given. Smoked turkey reduces oven load and preparation; carved in bite sizes for easy service.
	Special Touches: Nametags Place cards Gifts—Christmas Bible verse for each guest	Tables set with cloths, centerpieces, and a place setting of napkin, fork, and water glass.
	Small Christmas wreaths and votives in center on each table. Seating: Place cards on tables. There is a tendency for people to sit with the same familiar friends. Place cards help to mix guests and aid sociability.	One spoon served with dessert and coffee. Dessert flambéd and served at table.
Purchase List:	3 smoked turkeys 2 hams 3½ quarts giblet sauce (2 ounces per person) 7 quarts cornbread dressing (4 ounces per person, or 8 servings per quart, 32 ounces per quart.) 2 quarts cranberry relish (1 ounce per person) 1 case Belgian endive 1 case Bibb lettuce 1 case watercress 3 cans julienne beets (approximately 2 cups per can) 60 individual acorn squash 6 small loaves pumpkin bread 5 dozen croissants Ice cream for dessert pistachio ice cream black cherry ice cream pineapple sherbet	

Wedding Reception

Chances are you'll be involved in a wedding reception at some time. I like to keep these occasions simple and to the point. And if possible—crisis free. Unfortunately, this isn't always the case. For example, one of the many challenges I had as food director at The Houston Club was to get a magnificent four-tiered wedding cake to a member's home for a garden reception.

The chef and his young helpers traveled with the cake—in separate tiers—about 20 miles in an unairconditioned van on a very humid day! They watched in disbelief as the icing began to slip off one of the large tiers. The crew had extra icing for touch-ups to ensure a superior finished product; however, they didn't have enough to match the crisis.

Pressed for time, they stopped at a corner market and purchased some aerosol shaving cream. You guessed it. They covered the damaged area of the cake with shaving cream, making all the appropriate swirls and curls.

When they arrived at their destination, they assembled the cake and "volunteered" to cut and serve the delicate dish—very carefully, of course. The mother of the bride was delighted.

It has been more than 15 years since the incident and everyone at the reception seems to have escaped the obituary column. I therefore believe it's safe to say "All's well that ends well."

To many, the thought of planning a wedding reception is overwhelming. But it shouldn't be. If you'll follow the guidelines laid down here—and conduct further research if the situation warrants—you'll be able to stage a highly successful reception. And you're almost certain to find solace in the fact that further receptions will be infinitely easier to plan and stage.

The guidelines I'll set down apply to a "typical" wedding reception. To plan a more elaborate reception, or for further details on protocol, I recommend Amy Vanderbilt's *Complete Book on Etiquette.*

It's generally acceptable to hold the reception at a site of your choice: normally in your own home, at a country club, or your church. And this one caveat applies universally: If you plan to hold the reception outdoors, make alternate plans in case of inclement weather. For example, if you plan to hold your reception outside in the church "garden," be sure to have space reserved inside in case it rains.

A proper floor plan such as this will enable you to stage a highly successful wedding reception.

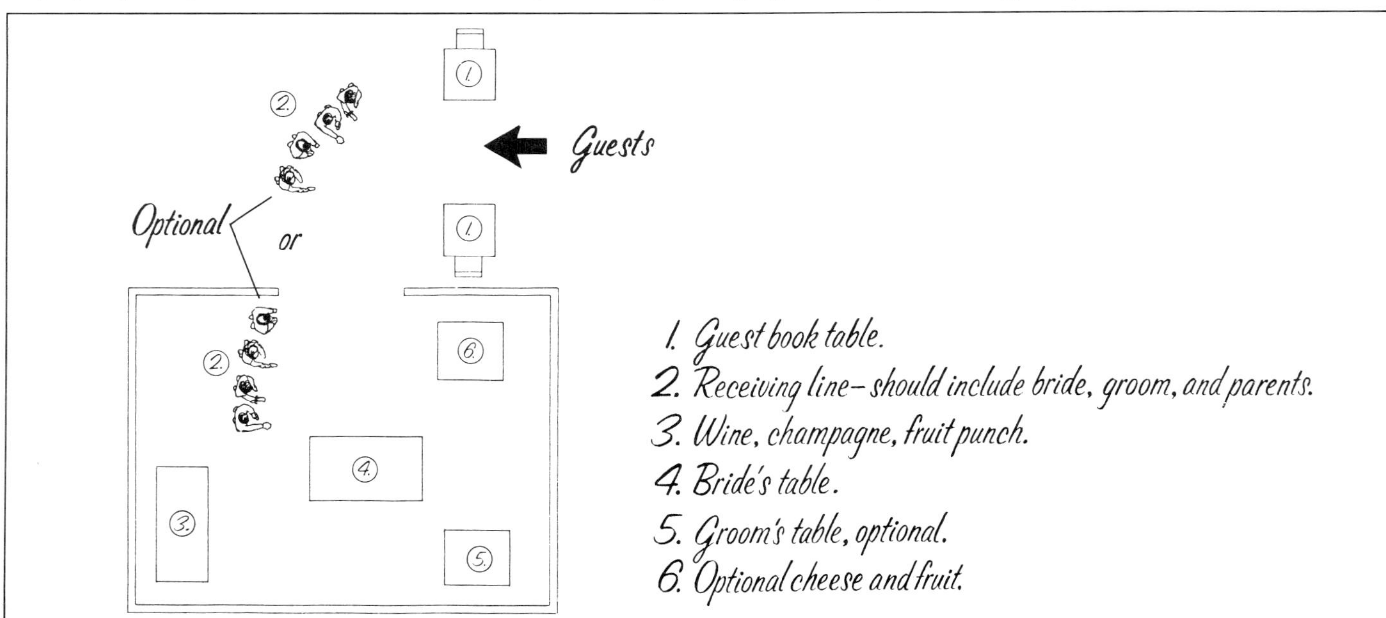

Whether you plan a small, informal reception, or a big, formal one is not especially important. What *is* important is that you plan a gay and festive party that will be a pleasant experience for everyone present.

Whom should you invite to the reception? It depends on the situation. If the reception is to be held immediately after the wedding, all guests present must naturally be invited. However, if the reception is to be staged at a later time and place—say, at a dinner party later in the evening—you obviously have the option of inviting only selected guests.

Regardless of where you decide to hold the reception, it's normally wise to engage the facility as far in advance as possible (see Chapter 2). When making your reservations, you'll want to check up on a number of things, such as: parking facilities, coat-checking facilities, rooms available in which bride and groom can change

Second only to the bride and groom in attention-getting is the wedding cake.

clothes; photo session(s), placement of receiving line, arrangement of tables, decorations, and menu. All party-planning rules referred to in Chapter 1 apply to the reception, whether it be a seated meal, a buffet, or stand-up affair.

Having the affair photographed is an extremely important activity, both at the wedding and the reception. I strongly suggest that you select a thoroughly professional photographer—one with whom you can communicate readily. Meet with him or her well in advance of the wedding and describe *specifically* the pictures *you* want taken. At the same time, make allowances for the photographer's being able to take any other pictures "on his own."

Generally, photographers will take pictures before and after the ceremony. Where practicable, I suggest you allow him to take as many pictures before the ceremony as possible. To avoid your guests having to wait too long it's best to plan exact pictures and inform some "take-charge" person in each family to help assemble them and expedite the photography.

Such waiting time can't be eliminated, only minimized. But the time can be made more pleasant for guests by serving champagne or punch before the receiving line forms. During the picture-taking, the bride should cut the wedding cake before the receiving line forms to speed up serving and again minimize waiting time (see Cake-Cutting and Serving).

The Receiving Line

The receiving line forms as soon as possible, in readiness for the arrival of the guests. Where possible, the line may be located *away* from the entrance to the reception room so guests will not have to wait outside the room. However, as long as you don't have people standing outside the building you may want to have the receiving line at the main entrance so people can pass through the line quickly, and thus shorten the wait for other guests. This generally makes the receiving line move faster, because having the line in the room tends to make it move leisurely and slow down the pace. The larger the reception the more concern you will have in making this decision.

The traditional receiving line moves guests from left to right so the bride can be on the groom's right.

In any event, I believe a minimum receiving line with the bride, groom, and the bride's parents, or at least the mothers of the bride and groom, is desirable. Though the receiving line may vary, it is courteous for the guests to be able to meet at least the parents as well as the bride and groom. Also, it avoids the frustrations for guests to have to identify the parents and then because of monopolized conversations wait to speak to the parents which evolves from a more informal gathering.

The traditional receiving line enables guests to pass from left to right so the bride may be on the bridegroom's right.

Everyone in the receiving line should be reminded to repeat each guest's name distinctly to the next person in line.

Menu

The choice of menus that can be served at a wedding reception is limitless. The items invariably included are the traditional wedding cake, champagne and fruit punch, mints and nuts. Options are the groom's cake, wine, cheese and fruit, or other food and beverages of your choice.

A champagne punch may be served and will reduce the cost substantially. Champagne fountains are exciting centerpieces but tend to waste champagne and eliminate the carbonation. As a result, you might want to use colored water and flowers in the fountain instead of champagne. Fruit punch should be provided for children and others who desire it.

For a large reception it is a good idea to have the champagne or wine on a separate table from the fruit punch. You can also have the beverages passed but in any case, start filling glasses and punch cups before the guests arrive. (See wedding reception floor plan, page 52.)

The Wedding Cake

The tiered wedding cake with white icing is traditional. It may have a chocolate, fruit, lemon, carrot, or other flavored tier covered with white icing to replace a separate groom's cake. In addition, it may be decorated with real flowers, delicately tinted icing flowers, wedding bells, or a miniature bride and groom. The top tier is often saved and frozen, then eaten later, usually on the first anniversary.

The bride's table, with the cake as the centerpiece, is often a separate table and should be prominently placed. Be sure to allow space for the bride and groom to be photographed as she cuts the cake.

In planning the size of the cake, you can estimate serving about two-thirds of the total guests invited to the reception. If you decide to order a groom's cake, order a big one, since this is often guests' favorite. If you fancy a wedding cake with more than three or so tiers (for beauty, not consumption), you can sometimes order "dummy" decorated tiers.

Cake-Cutting and Serving

The cake-cutting is a ceremony in itself. The bride stands at the groom's right, and, with a cake knife decorated with white ribbon, cuts the first slice from the bottom tier. The groom may assist in the cake-cutting by placing his hand over hers. The bride then breaks the slice in half and shares it with the groom, symbolizing their sharing life together. The cake is then cut—either by a friend or by a professional helper—in relatively small slices from the bottom up. The cake may be served on paper luncheon-size or cocktail napkins, or plates. Forks may be used.

Decorations

Decorations can contribute much to the beauty and distinction of the wedding and reception. Thus, the first step is to discuss your ideas with a florist or party designer, and coordinate them with the club, hotel, or church. Experts in these facilities can usually help you do your planning. For instance, you may or may not want to use table cloths for the cake and punch tables depending on the tables. You will need sizes of tables to be used for planning decorations and table cloths. Often items furnished by such facilities include candelabra, punch bowls, table cloths, and special draped effects that look terrific but will save you some expense.

Considerations for the reception decorations are decorated cake knife, bride's cake table, groom's cake table, punch table, (not necessarily separate table) other food tables, small cocktail size tables for guests to sit at or place drinks on (in the event you're having a meal or substantial food you will need centerpieces for these tables). Wedding napkins, matches, (optional to print with bride and groom's name) should be included in your plans. Other decorations may be used at the entrance, or walls, ceiling, or outside.

For the bride's book table(s), a bridesmaid's bouquet can serve as an excellent decoration. For a large reception, buy a bride's book that has removable pages, so two tables can be used to expedite the procedure. Don't forget to have pens available.

Flower petals (fresh or paper), confetti, rice and bird seed can be used to throw on the newlyweds as they depart. Caution should be taken in using rice and birdseed, since they might be thrown in someone's eye or cause a fall.

Music

Music is optional at the reception. A harp, string trio, piano, or recorded music is a lovely addition for any type or size reception. For dancing, a five-piece (or larger) group may be used.

Tossing the Bouquet

As the bride and groom leave to change into their traveling clothes, the bride signals her attendants to gather around a stairway, balcony, or any convenient spot. She then tosses her bouquet into the group. Tradition says that the lucky girl who catches it will be the next to marry.

Wedding Reception

Phase I—The Beginning

Activities		Considerations
Decide	Date: Wedding date Time:	Following the wedding allow time for pictures to be taken and transportation, if necessary, to the reception location. Remember, you only have one chance at these pictures. Think ahead of time of relatives, friends, etc. that you especially want photographed and give a list to your photographer.
	Location:	Be sure you have ample room with satisfactory dressing rooms available.
	Budget:	
	Guest list:	Supplied by the bride and groom. Invitations sent by bride's family.
Confirm	Caterers	For cakes, food and other services.
	Services	Florists–music Servers, attendants, photographer, tables, chairs, china, silver, punch bowl, cups and glasses. (Champagne, fruit punch, napkins and table cloths.)
Order	Invitations	Usually included with wedding invitation.

Phase II—You're on Your Way

Activities		Considerations
Plan	Food: Bride's cake Groom's cake Mints Nuts Beverages Punch Champagne	Candelabra, plates, forks and napkins

Phase III—The Specifics

Make list	Mints Nuts Napkins

Activities		Considerations
	Matches Candles Cakes Flowers-decorations Punch ingredients Champagne Rice Bride's Book	

Accommodating Overnight Guests

Make everything casual. Help your guests feel free to participate and feel at ease.

Make a list, such as the checklists that follow. Try to think of everything your guests might need plus nice extras to make them feel special.

One must generally plan proper entertainment for guests. Guests cannot be expected to know what fits into the host's schedule or capabilities. One may, of course, give guests options, but the ideas must come from the host.

Suggestions for breakfast, which can be served in the dining room, or where guests can help themselves, include:

Fresh melons with berries
Sweet rolls
Date bread
Coffee
Cereal, milk

Checklists for Overnight Guests

When setting up the dining room for breakfast, include:

1. Placemats
2. Napkins
3. Silverware
4. Fresh flowers in center
5. Candles
6. China
7. Cup and saucer, dinner plate on table (see basic place setting in Chapter 1)
8. Glasses on table
9. Any written instructions for guests.

Prepare the kitchen for overnight guests by including:

1. Coffee (already set up)
2. Pitcher of water in refrigerator
3. Silver biscuit dish for date bread and sweet rolls
4. Sugar/cream/milk
5. Jelly/butter
6. Menu

Suggestions for the guest room:

1. Fresh fruit or mixed dried fruit
2. Fresh flowers or plants
3. Fresh soap and towels
4. Tissues and toilet paper
5. Spare toothbrush, toothpaste
6. Current magazines and newspapers
7. Pleasantly scented candles, matches
8. Welcome signs ("We're glad you are here!")
9. Ice water
10. Proper hangers, drawers, and closet space
11. Shampoo and shower cap
12. Lotion and powder
13. Aspirin
14. Clock, radio
15. Clean, neat room
16. Post cards or stationery
17. Turn down the bed with flower on pillow
18. Tourist information from your local motel or Chamber of Commerce
19. Tell guests to help themselves and to feel free to make their own beds or whatever.

Chapter Four

Adding "Show Biz" to Your Parties

Flambé

"Sell the *sizzle,* not the steak," super salesman Elmer Wheeler told us a generation ago. That sizzle is *showmanship,* the extra flair that turns the ordinary into the spectacular, and in the process, adds a touch of class.

The culinary arts has its own special—and literal—"sizzle." It's called *flambé cookery,* or the art of cooking with flame.

Flambéing can be inexpensive; it gives you a chance to impress on a limited budget. It's easy to do; you can "perform" right in your own home. And it's easy to learn (though some specials do take lots of practice). It can crown all your efforts for an enchanting evening. Flames can be the *pièce de résistance*! There is glamour and showmanship in serving a flaming chateaubriand, fruit jubilee, or Café Brulot Diabolique.

There are a host of other extraordinary dishes in this chapter. These dishes are, for the most part, world renowned. They have been adapted from dishes concocted by the top chefs and professionals in some of the world's most respected hotels and restaurants. I have also added a few simple methods of my own creation. The showmanship ideas include recipes for cooking or making a salad in front of guests; flaming only in front of guests; igniting in kitchen and presenting for guests to see; and very simple flaming ideas with candles and alcohol-soaked cotton squares. The recipes are wonderful, even if you don't flame them in front of the guests.

Indeed, food professionals are forever outdoing each other in this spectacular art form. In fact, it was this keen sense of competitiveness that caused one of my most embarrassing moments as a food professional. The incident again emphasizes the need to be prepared for almost anything when hosting a party.

In this case, a dear friend, a leading home economist, asked me to show her garden club how to flambé. Since it was a special occasion, I took an experienced professional maitre'd along to make sure we would have a successful demonstration.

After rhapsodizing at length over the virtues of flambéing, the maitre'd and I tried to show guests how easy it was to flame some bananas. Nothing happened! We both tried every trick in the book to induce a flame. Still, no luck; not even a spark.

What caused the "flame-out?" Well, the demonstration took place at a *competitor's* country club. We had relied on *their* maitre'd to furnish the flambé cart and alcohol. They did. But the brandies and alcohol had been watered!

Moral: It takes lots of practice and preparation to flame expertly. I might even suggest a few dry-runs before you perform for your guests.

Flaming Instructions

To set up a flambé table or cart, all you need is:

1. Alcohol burner or sterno heat unit, chafing dish

2. Saute pan (shallow skillet)
3. Matches
4. Brandy, alcohol, liqueurs
5. Service spoon
6. Napkin (damp cloth)
7. Sauce or butter, and ingredients for presentation

Also, check the recipe and be ready with serving dishes, garnishes, and any additional foods to be served at the same time.

Arrange items on cart or table to ensure strong eye appeal. Add them to chafing dish one at a time. Use crystal cruets or pretty containers on cart for brandy and liqueurs.

Before giving you details on how to flambé some world-famous dishes, let me pass on a few safety precautions and a few tips on intensifying the "food drama."

* Proceed carefully at all times, but especially when carrying flambé items and when lighting the dish. Sparklers are often used; however, be aware that the sparks can light on your guests' clothes and leave holes, if not flame the guest. They are best used outdoors for show and not near the guests. (They may also mar the china and your linens.) In any case, keep a wet napkin handy! Avoid cooking in drafts from windows, doors, and fans. And be certain the surfaces are fireproof in the immediate surroundings, including equipment.

* The secret of flaming is the alcohol content and its temperature. Alcoholic content must be 100 proof to ignite at room temperature. Thus, if the proof is less—such as in the case of brandy—it must be heated and then set aflame. Warm the brandy; warm the pouring utensil; light with a taper or long match.

* Everclear (grain alcohol—190 proof) is often used in a small ovenproof container, an empty egg shell, or an orange or lemon basket in supplying the blaze of glory. Insert the container in the items you wish to set ablaze by hiding it in the dish so the container doesn't show. For a miniature "volcano," put the container in the center top of a plum pudding, an ice cream mold, a cake, or a pyramid of ice, and then ignite the alcohol and let it burn. Or, encircle the dessert with orange or lemon baskets filled with a flammable liquid. Also, you can soak cotton squares in the alcohol, place them around items on a tray, on a skewer, or in lemon baskets or glass containers. This contains the flames but creates the effect. (See "Ice Cream Molds" later in this chapter.) Everclear is strictly for a flame flourish, and should not be used on the food itself, as it changes the flavor of food. The very simplest form of flaming can be accomplished with a candle. (See recipe for Pineapple Holiday Dessert, page 64 or Paté with Candles, page 80.)

* Also, turn out the lights for full effect. You may want to show the flaming dish by parading it among the guests before serving. You can add other acts in the parade (use your imagination) from monkeys, to fiddlers, to acrobats, to a costumed dancer. Experience is the best teacher. Practice is an absolute must for making a flaming dish before your guests. And, though many delicious dishes may be served in a flaming way, I suggest you do just one for any single occasion.

The following are recipes to get you started. From the very dramatic Café Brulot recipe, which definitely takes practice, to the simple methods which need little practice, you can copy the experts from San Francisco to Paris!

Café Brulot Diabolique

This luxurious spiced beverage was created by the master French Chef Brillot-Savarin. The magic of it climaxes in an orange corkscrew of flame. It serves 8–10 demitasse cups.

On cart: chafing dish with deep pan, wooden spoon, fork, and sharp knife.
1/2 jigger Kirschwasser (a colorless cherry brandy)
1 jigger dark rum
1 jigger brandy
1 whole orange
1 stick cinnamon

5 whole cloves plus 12 for orange spiral
6 teaspoons sugar
3 cups hot black coffee

In front of guests:

1. Mingle Kirsch, rum, cinnamon stick, cloves and sugar in pan.
2. Peel orange in spiral (see Food Carving, page 76).
3. Light fire under pan.
4. Stick 12 whole cloves in orange peel, 1/2 inch apart.
5. Stir mixture and remove cinnamon stick from pan to avoid bitterness.
6. Place orange peel in warm liquid.
7. Pour brandy over peel and ignite.
8. Pick up end of orange peel with fork and hold high over pan, moving it up and down. Continue flames with more brandy.
9. As flames decrease, add coffee.
10. Stir, remove orange peel and serve in demitasse or diablo cups.

Café Brulot

A simple version for the same coffee finale: add 2 tablespoons sugar, break in cinnamon stick, a vanilla bean (or 1 teaspoon vanilla extract), thinly peeled orange rind in chafing dish and stir. Add 1/2 cup warm brandy, stir and ignite. As the flames dance in dish, add 3 cups hot black coffee. Remove orange rind and vanilla bean. Serve in demitasse cups. Do not serve with cream or sugar.

Flaming Blueberries and Fresh Sliced Peaches
(serves 6)

2 1/2 cups fresh sliced peaches
2 1/2 cups fresh blueberries
2 tablespoons lemon juice
1/2 cup apricot brandy

You may use the following ingredients in all flaming fruit dessert recipes:

8 tablespoons butter
1 cup sugar
1 1/2 lemons
2 juicy oranges
4 tablespoons Curacao (orange flavored liqueur, may also use Triple-Sec, Grand Marnier or Cointreau)
2 tablespoons Kirschwasser
2 tablespoons brandy

Place butter in warm sauté pan or chafing dish and melt. Add sugar and stir over heat until dissolved. Wrap orange and lemon in clean linen napkin (or cover with cheese cloth and tie with pretty ribbons or bells) and squeeze juice into pan. Continue cooking until syrupy.

Place peaches and blueberries in sauce and stir gently until heated. For flaming, add approximately 1/2 cup warm brandy and ignite, pour over peach or vanilla ice cream or crepe suzettes. (Ice cream should be in heatproof dishes.)

Cherries Jubilee

Make ahead of time: seeded bing cherries (8 per serving)

Put cherries in pan and cover with syrup from can, add 2 teaspoons red currant jelly, 2 teaspoons honey, cover pan and bring to near boil. Before guests: add warm cherry mixture to chafing dish and heat. Add Curacao, a little rum and brandy, ignite and serve over vanilla ice cream or cheese cake.

Banana Flambé
(two servings per banana)

Peel banana and slice (you may use waffle cutter). Sprinkle with granulated sugar. In hot sauté pan put 2 tablespoons of butter and 2 tablespoons of honey. Add a few drops of lemon juice and 2 ounces of orange juice. Add 1/2 ounce Grand Marnier and heat. Place banana slices in pan; bring to a near boil. Pour bit of brandy and rum over them, ignite and serve blazing over pound cake or coffee ice cream.

Pears Flambé

Pear halves stuffed with macaroons and soaked overnight in Grand Marnier, for flambé. Place in chafing dish. Heat, sprinkle with brandy, let the brandy warm, and ignite. For variations, add sliced almonds, toasted coconut chips, or chopped mixed candied fruit to macaroons.

Crepe Suzettes

Basic Crepes

7/8 cup flour
1/4 cup sugar
3 eggs
1/8 teaspoon vanilla
2 tablespoons melted butter, pinch of salt

Sift together flour and sugar. Add eggs, one at a time, vanilla and salt, beat with wire whisk. Add butter and enough milk to give batter the consistency of heavy cream, beating with wire whisk until smooth. Let stand half hour in refrigerator.

Barely coat pan with batter and cook. Make into small pancakes about 4 to 4 1/2 inches in size, on well buttered pan. When done on one side, slide out of pan onto plate and place uncooked side down, then back into pan and cook. Have large sheet of brown paper handy on which to toss pancakes as they are done. Do not let them become crisp. The brown paper absorbs the excess cooking butter. These cakes are very thin. Prepare 2 for each person. They may be wrapped in waxed paper for freezing.

Sauce for Crepe Suzettes
(serves 6, 2 crepes each)

8 tablespoons butter
1 cup sugar
1 1/2 lemons
2 oranges

Place butter in sauté pan and melt. Add sugar and stir over heat until dissolved. Wrap oranges and lemon halves in clean linen napkin and squeeze juice in sauté pan. Continue cooking until syrupy. Add:

4 tablespoons Grand Marnier
2 tablespoons Kirschwasser
4 tablespoons brandy

Place crepes in sauce and roll. For flaming: add 4 jiggers brandy, light and serve.

Crepes Surprise
(make in advance)

Roll cooled crepes around your favorite ice cream or fruit and place on tray in freezer, well covered or wrapped in foil. Serve with your favorite sauce compatible with ice cream flavor. Take out of freezer about 15 minutes before serving. May also flame by heating and flaming sauce (see page 66 for quick sauces).

Spectacular Desserts

Pineapple Volcano
(serves 2, make a day in advance)

1 large ripe pineapple
1/4 cup dark rum
8–10 almond macaroons, crumbled
1/2 cup apricot preserves
2 scoops vanilla or coffee ice cream
1/4 cup 151-proof rum (see Flaming Instructions)

Split pineapple in half, lengthwise. Remove fruit from shell, being careful not to pierce the shell. (Use grapefruit knife to scoop out.) Discard core and reserve shell. Cut pineapple meat into 1-inch cubes. Mix with macaroons and preserves. Pour dark rum over mixture and let stand for at least 30 minutes in refrigerator or do the day before and keep well covered. When ready to serve, fill shell with pineapple mixture, top with ice cream. To flame, in sauté pan ignite 1/4 cup rum with match (do not heat rum). Pour flaming rum over ice cream and pineapple. Serve immediately while burning. Don't forget to turn the lights out before your show. Parade around room for guests to see. This can also be served like Baked Alaska by covering with meringue. Insert small heat-proof container in top of meringue to hold alcohol for flaming.

Meringue for Baked Alaska or Pineapple Volcano

5 large egg whites
1 teaspoon salt

1/2 teaspoon vanilla
1/4 teaspoon cream of tartar
10 tablespoons sugar

Add salt to egg whites and beat until foamy. Beat in sugar 1 tablespoon at a time. Beat until egg whites stand in stiff peaks. Add vanilla. Beat and spread over pineapple. Recipe will cover one 9-inch cake pan for Alaska or 8 servings. You may also make your ice box pies sky high and serve in a flaming manner.

Baked Alaska

Cover your cake, fruit, and ice cream with a thick meringue, building the dessert into a spiral peak. Brown the meringue in an oven, place dessert on a serving dish (large) and flame with brandy and alcohol. Often, chefs use a blow torch for browning.

Ice Cream Fancies

These are simple desserts with endless variations and opportunities for showmanship at its best.

Ice Cream Ring
(serves 12–14)

1/2 gallon vanilla ice cream
2 cups your favorite preserves (cherry, peach, strawberry)
1 cup toffee candy or almond macaroons or nuts
1 cup brandy or bourbon

Mix all ingredients together, pour in bundt cake mold (previously sprayed with vegetable oil) and place in freezer. Let freeze.

When ready to serve, defrost by placing warm towel on pan and turn out on tray. Decorate with fruit (candied or otherwise) or nuts. For a birthday, use candles. For holidays, place holly around tray and garnish with cranberries. Use flambé to present to guests and then cut and serve. (Extra servings may be cut from extra rings in kitchen.) For Christmas entertaining, use pistachio, black cherry ice cream and pineapple sherbet instead of vanilla ice cream. Instead of mixing all together, make in layers. (See Ice Cream Mold and flambé of this in the next recipe.)

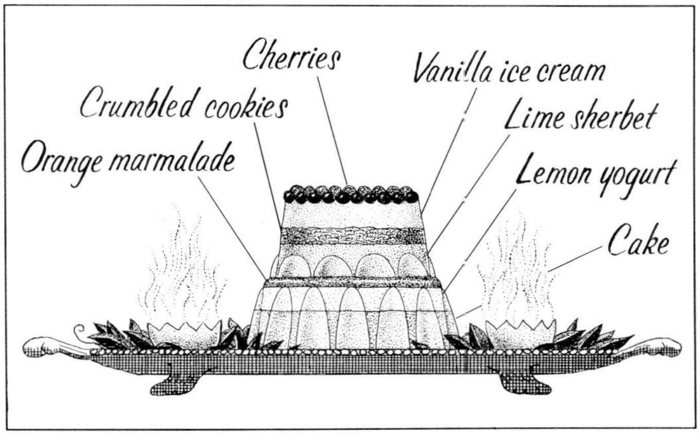

The variety of ingredients and layers of an ice cream mold flambé let you "tailor" it to any occasion or guest.

Ice Cream Molds—Multiflavored

Ice cream molds are easy to make and can be made ahead of time. Use your favorite shaped container for putting in freezer.

1. Prepare mold pan with vegetable oil or spray. *Remember,* what you put in the mold first will be the top of the dessert.
2. Use your favorite ice cream, sherbet, or frozen yogurt. Let it defrost slightly and make a layer in the pan and freeze.
3. Other layers may be added. Allow each layer to harden before adding the next. Here are suggested layer variations; be sure to choose compatible flavors:

   fruit (frozen raspberries, strawberries)
   preserves or jams
   crumbled cookies (filled types, fig newtons)
   crumbled toffee candy
   caramel sauces mixed with nuts
   chocolate sauce mixed with crumbs or
   chocolate chips (may melt)
   cake
   nuts

4. The topping or decorations for the mold can be placed in the pan first, or you can quickly decorate after you unmold it. Have everything ready.

5. Place mold in center of large tray for a flaming presentation. In greenery around tray hide small heat-proof dishes or lemon baskets with grain alcohol soaked cotton squares. Place them where you won't ignite the person carrying or presenting the dish to guests.
6. When ready to present, ignite, turn lights down, and flame away.

Ice Cream Sky High Pie

For ice cream sky high pie, fill gingersnap, walnut or graham cracker pie crust with your favorite ice cream. Add meringue topping or top with your favorite sauce, layer of lemon sherbet or fresh strawberries. (See meringue for Baked Alaska pages 62–63.) When adding meringue, brown top, place in freezer until ready to serve.

Snifter Pretties

Roll pistachio ice cream ball in toasted coconut chips. Make ahead and place in freezer. When ready to serve add butterscotch or caramel sauce to bottom of brandy snifter and put pistachio ball on top and serve.

Variations for snifter:

1. Roll vanilla ice cream in pecans, serve with chocolate sauce.
2. Roll peppermint ice cream in shredded coconut, serve with mint sprig and a little crème de menthe.
3. Make a ball of half vanilla and half strawberry ice cream, serve with fresh strawberry sauce.
4. Use assorted small scoops of ice creams and/or sherbets.
5. Strawberry sherbet—mix pineapple sherbet with fresh strawberries, drop of red food coloring and behold, a beauty!

Flavored Whipped Cream

Beat 1 cup heavy cream until frothy. Gradually add 1/3 cup confectioner's sugar and desired flavoring. Continue to beat until cream is of desired consistency. Use as a contrasting flavor for desserts.

Liqueur flavorings:

1 tablespoon crème de noyaux
2 tablespoons crème de menthe or oil of peppermint
1 tablespoon curacao and 2 teaspoons grated orange rind
2 tablespoons peach liqueur and 1/4 teaspoon almond extract

Pineapple Holiday Dessert

(serves 8, may be made the day before.)

This is good for any occasion and can be decorated accordingly—for Valentine's Day, 4th of July, or Christmas. It is fun and easy.

1/2 gallon pineapple sherbet
4 whole fresh pineapples cut in half, cored and fresh meat scooped out (See Food Carving for instructions)
1 (10-ounce) package whole fresh cranberries washed,
dash red food coloring as desired

Mix fresh pineapple, cranberries, and sherbet together in blender or food processor and add color last. Fill pineapple half with cranberry-sherbet mixture and place each half in freezer. Put remaining sherbet back in carton and put in freezer until sherbet in pineapple has set (frozen). Then add scoop of sherbet on top. Add fresh holly and candle inside of pineapple by using toothpick or ice pick to make holes. When ready to serve remove from freezer 30 minutes ahead of time. Turn off lights and present candle-lighted individual dessert on plate. You may also add snowman, Santa Claus, or other fancy party pick to concoction.

Fairy Floss (Cotton Candy) Dessert

If you live in a low humidity area and can buy cotton candy wrapped air-tight on a stick or paper cone you have a memorable dessert. It should be purchased not more than 24 hours in advance and kept in a cool, dry area in a plastic bag. I have kept it several days but don't push your luck.

This delightful creation shows how cotton candy can be used with a pineapple basket, sherbet, and fresh berries to make a heavenly dessert.

Try this for a children's party, ladies' luncheon, or an important dinner party. Place cotton candy on plate in nest. Add ice cream ball in center. Pistachio ice cream is pretty, or if you have several assorted colors and flavors, make small balls ahead of time and place in freezer. When ready to serve, add assorted ice cream or sherbet balls to cotton candy and serve. May be topped with fresh berries, or substitute berries for ice cream.

Strawberries for Buffet or Individual Dessert

Giant strawberries should be clean, capped (cut on bottom so they will sit), and hollowed with melon ball scoop. Fill with flavored whipped cream with your pastry tube. (May tint and flavor with food coloring and perhaps oil of peppermint.) To decorate petit fours and tarts, use red colored apple jelly.

Strawberries Romanoff
(serves 8)

2 pints fresh strawberries
1 cup confectioners' sugar
1 cup heavy cream
1 teaspoon almond extract
2 tablespoons Cointreau or Grand Marnier

Hull strawberries, wash in cold water and drain carefully. In medium bowl, sprinkle sugar over berries and toss gently with liqueur. Refrigerate 1 hour, stirring occasionally. In chilled bowl, with rotary beater, whip cream until stiff. Add almond extract. Fold into strawberries. Serve at once.

Elegant Mousses

For elegant mousses, use vanilla ice cream and add desired flavor by mixing with preserves, jam, jellies, marmalades, almond paste, or candied marrons (chestnuts).

Apricot Alexander Mousse
(serves 6)

1 16-ounce can apricot halves, drained
2 cups vanilla ice cream
3 ounces brandy or rum (optional)
3 ounces crème de cacao (optional)

Place all ingredients in blender, blend until smooth. Pour into glass, garnish with nuts, toasted coconut chips, or make an individual flower on top of each mousse with apricot slivers, and a candied citron (red or green) center. You may place in the freezer or serve immediately.

Simple Preparation Ideas

Use preserves, jams, jellies, and marmalades for quick sauces, hot or cold hors d'oeuvres, meats, and for sundae toppings. For orange sauce, use orange marmalade. (For duckling, ham sauce, or dessert, when mixed with lemon or orange sherbet.)

For cranberry sauce, use cranberry jelly.

For cherry sauce, use cherry jelly or preserves.

Use fig preserves in ice cream mold, or spread between cake layers.

For Brazilian sauce, mix pineapple, bananas, pecans, coconut, and rum together. Heat in chicken consommé and add to ham or Canadian bacon.

Meats

Flaming Chateaubriand
(serves 4, 8-ounce portions.)

cooked, beef tender (2 lbs raw)
meat drippings 1/8 cup butter
salt and pepper mill
1/2 cup red burgundy wine
1/4 cup brandy
grain alcohol
carving board, fork and knife
dinner plates and garnish

Chateaubriand is the center cut of beef tenderloin. Mostly cook tenderloin in kitchen before bringing into dining area for flaming. Add meat drippings and butter in sauté pan. Before guests, sprinkle tenderloin with salt and cracked pepper and place in pan. Add wine. Pour brandy over meat and a dash of grain alcohol in pan (not on meat). Ignite. Allow alcohol to burn off—flavor remains. Carve and serve as soon as flame dies down. Have vegetables ready to go on plates or passed immediately.

Breast of Chicken Flambé

Bake chicken breasts prior to arrival of guests. In the presence of your guests, rub inside of sauté pan with garlic bean. Add 2 tablespoons butter for each breast and heat to bubbling. Season with a little lemon juice and 1/8 cup chicken bouillon per breast. Place chicken breasts in sauce until piping hot.

Pour brandy over chicken; set aflame. When flame dies down serve at once. Garnish with toasted almonds and serve on saffron rice (yellow) with spiced red apple ring or slices.

Chicken Martinique

Saute: *1/2 cup chopped bacon*

Add: *1/2 cup chopped ham; 1/2 cup green pepper and onion, diced small; 1/2 cup tomato paste.*

Simmer above ingredients for approximately 5 minutes. Then add: *1 pint heavy cream; dash salt and white pepper; 1 1/4 ounce Jamaica rum.*

Add: *2 pounds cooked chicken, diced to Martinique sauce.*

To avoid the ubiquitous patty shell or holland rusk, serve in a fresh coconut half or pineapple boat. For coconut half, have your grocer cut coconut in half with meat saw and trim bottom of each half so it will sit on plate. Preheat oven to 350°. Spoon chicken into coconut shell and place in oven to heat through. Serve immediately. Use same procedure for pineapple. Crabmeat or shrimp may be used in place of chicken. The recipe won't know the difference.

This dish shows how the "Heart of Texas" style can be used with boneless chicken breasts. The yellow squash crowns may be filled with asparagus, as in this case, or with spinach.

Leftovers with Class

Alaska Casserole
(serves 6)

6 cups cubed, cooked meat: chicken, turkey, ham, tuna, king crabmeat, beef or a combination of your choice
1 cup mayonnaise
1 cup sour cream or yogurt
1 tablespoon lemon juice
1 tablespoon finely chopped onion
1/2 teaspoon curry powder, or another spice of your choice
1/8 teaspoon cayenne pepper
1 cup green peas (frozen and thawed)
2 1/2 cups (1/2 pound) shredded Fontina or Havarti (Danish cheese)

In a large bowl, blend mayonnaise, sour cream, lemon juice, onion, curry, and cayenne pepper. Fold in peas, meat, and cheese. Spoon into buttered, shallow casserole dish; cover, bake in preheated oven at 300° for about 20 minutes and then remove for Alaska topping and return to oven for browning.

Alaska for Entree

In the early days of my career, I used this idea on eggs benedict for St. Patrick's Day. The mistake I made was in slightly tinting the meringue green, and since it was a special breakfast surprise party, you can well imagine their surprise. The Canadian bacon cut in a shamrock on top of the meringue helped them overcome their surprise but those green clouds nearly overcame the guests. So, beware!

For One Casserole or Six Clouds

For a festive touch, add a soft pillowy cloud of meringue to your casserole or individual entree.

6 egg whites
1/2 teaspoon cream of tartar
2 cups shredded white hard cheese (Swiss or monterrey)

Beat egg whites with cream of tartar until stiff peaks form. Gradually sprinkle and fold in cheese. Remove casserole or individual entrees from oven 8 to 10 minutes before baking period is completed. Spoon meringue onto warm mixture, forming 6 or 8 mounds, or spread over individual items like icing for Alaska. Return to oven at 400° until meringue is golden brown (8 to 10 minutes). Garnish with chopped parsley and paprika around edges. Serve at once.

Sliced Breast of Turkey "Heart of Texas Style"

Lay turkey on rice or asparagus. Top with heart-shaped Canadian bacon (or star-shaped for Christmas). Add cheese or mornay sauce, brown, and serve.

Lamb Chop

Split single 2-rib lamb chop to look like a horseshoe. Add meat stuffing (See London Beef Roll recipe on page 86) on top and dot with button mushrooms. Bake for approximately 45 minutes at 350°. Note: You may make your own paper frills or use ribbons.

The Posh Squash

As I sat alone at my desk
Pondering the menus ahead,
From the vegetables I heard a voice
And this is what it said.

I'm tired of being just plain squash.
Give me a chance—you'll see.
I'm always boiled, or stewed, or fried.
Let me show you what I can be!

With a slice here and there and a certain touch,
His being began to change

To flower, a crown, and a beautiful swan
And a centerpiece that I could arrange.

I took his advice and let me share
The fun of using the squash,
You'll never again think he's plain and dull,
He's versatile, unique, and quite posh!

Kissing Swans

One of the most versatile decorations for a party tray buffet, or seated meal, features "kissing swans" made of yellow squash. This is a perfect theme for a shower, a party honoring a bride and groom, anniversary, or any other occasion. They can be made the day before, placed on a tray, covered, and refrigerated. Here's how to do a pair of kissing swans. Use 3 crook-neck yellow squash; 4 whole cloves; 4 toothpicks—broken in half (8 pieces).

1. Squash must be carefully selected with distinct crook-necks, long "beaks" if possible and equal in size. Wash and dry.
2. Cut crook-necks diagonally on 2 squash.

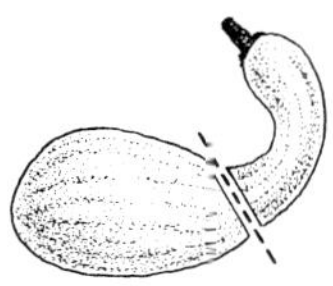

3. Reverse the heads and attach to squash with toothpicks. Slice bottom of each squash in an oval, so it will not roll over.

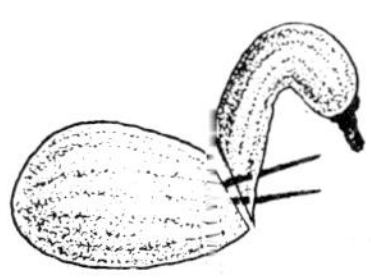

4. Use oval slice to make a tail feather.
5. Insert tail in end of squash by making thin insert with sharp pointed knife. May be reinforced with toothpick.
6. Cut beak. Make tiny split in beak for "lips" with tip of knife. Make eye with whole cloves. Don't panic; if you don't have any cloves, use an eyebrow pencil or felt-tip pen.

7. Third Squash—cut four matching ovals from each side of the third squash, "feather the wing" by making parallel cuts in each oval.

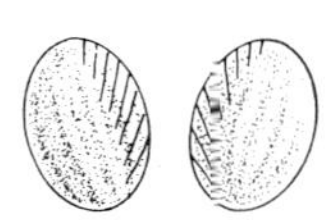

8. With a sharp pointed knife make a thin cut in each side of the swans and put in wings. Reinforce with toothpicks.

9. Place swans facing each other on the blue gelatin lake (see following).

Variations

1. Kissing swans may be placed with greenery on the center of your table. Yellow gourds, greenery (magnolia or loquat leaves are great), and the yellow swans are a pretty centerpiece. Use small wedding bells on ribbon around the swan's necks.
2. Make a swan family. Two large and two small swans.
3. Place on tray and surround with hors d'oeuvres.

Lake for Kissing Swans
(make in advance)

2 tablespoons unflavored gelatin (2 envelopes)
1 cup boiling water
1 cup cold water
drops of blue food coloring

Dissolve gelatin in hot water, add cold water and blue color. Mix. Pour in 9-inch cake pan that has been sprayed with vegetable oil. Place in refrigerator until firm. Unmold on tray just before serving and place squash swans on top.

For a different garnish for buffet centerpiece, use same recipe with light colors to match your decor and pour in rectangle or square pan and cut in cubes to edge or trim tray. You may also use cookie cutters for other designs.

To make your own designs, cut your own pattern out of paper. Place the pattern on the congealed gelatin. With a knife heated in hot water, cut around your pattern. Remove paper. This is especially good for letters and numbers and can be used for cake decorations.

Stuffed Squash (yellow or zucchini)
(serves 6, two halves each)

Clean and wash 6 squash. To make boats, cut squash in half lengthwise. To make crowns, cut squash into 1-inch-thick horizontal slices. Scoop out centers with spoon or melon ball cutter.

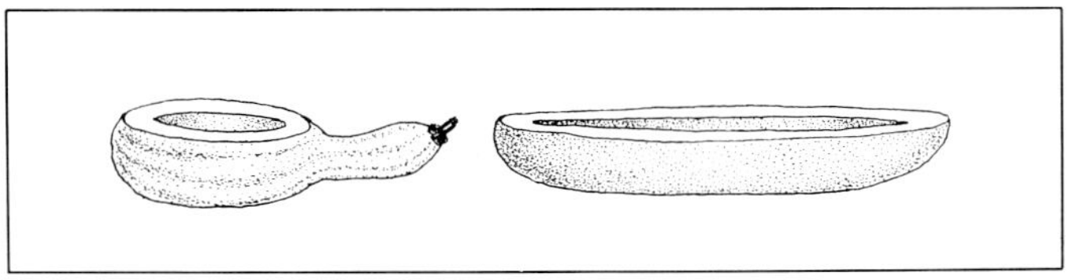

Cook shells in a small amount of boiling water, covered until tender. Use the meat stuffing, see recipe page 87 and brown in a skillet. Stuff in shells, sprinkle with Parmesan cheese and brown under broiler a few seconds.

Other Ideas for Baking Squash

Squash may be filled with beet puree, flavored with anise.

Baked zucchini and yellow squash slices may be filled with cheese and picante sauce, or zucchini or yellow squash crowns filled with cheese, top with cauliflower or broccoli.

Other Distinguished Vegetable Ideas

* Tomato crown with broccoli floweret.
* Tomato crown with fennel seed.
* Cherry tomato halves filled with green peas.
* Green peas with water chestnuts.
* Tiny whole carrots and rosebud beets. (Cook carrots and beets separately and mix just before serving.)
* Carrots with seedless grapes or spiced cranberries.
* Beets sauteed in Curacao butter and slivers of orange peel.
* Broccoli or cauliflower with mandarin oranges and pistachio nuts. (Warm oranges separately and add last to avoid discoloring broccoli.)
* Fresh mushroom caps filled with artichoke hearts, hollandaise sauce.
* Acorn squash baked with spinach souffle.
* Acorn squash baked with filling of spiced stewed apples, raisins, walnuts, topped with yogurt or cheese.
* Add currants to saffron rice.
* Add mincemeat to rice—5 cups rice to 1 cup mincemeat.
* Noodle nest—toss together 4 cans Chinese noodles and 2 egg whites. Shape and bake.
* Place 2½ cups cooked fresh asparagus spears standing up in a small tart shell. (See recipe for tart shells, page 85.) Tie the spears with a slender green onion stem and stuff mushrooms in shell around asparagus. Put in oven to heat and serve.

* Leftover vegetables can often be pureed (in blender or food processor). Add sauces such as taco, Worcestershire, cheese or flavor with your favorite spice. Garnish! Heat and serve. The possible combinations are endless and some of your best recipes can be concocted. Use crushed bran flakes for a crumb topping.

Houston Club Gingerbread

The specialty we had at the famous Houston Club during my tenure there wasn't an exotic dish at all. It was plain old gingerbread! Only it wasn't too *plain*, and it rarely got to be *old*. Members and guests still consume it daily in huge quantities.

What makes the Houston Club gingerbread such an overwhelming success? Many board members and inquisitive guests tried to find out the secret ingredients. Even the redoubtable *Gourmet Magazine* was unable to obtain the heralded recipe from our chef.

The secret was locked securely in the head of the chef who concocted it. And he prepared his specialty daily under "security" every bit as tight as that at Los Alamos.

Chefs who create these culinary delights are often like artists. They take a great deal of "pride of authorship" in their creative efforts.

As a result, some of these secrets never get passed on. The creator of the Houston Club gingerbread confided his secret on his final day before he retired. He hinted that he made his famous gingerbread from a *precious blend of leftover desserts*!

Whiskey Pecan Cake

Another incident at the Houston Club illustrates just how far some chefs will go to "protect" their specialty.

In this case, a columnist for one of Houston's largest newspapers wanted to run a recipe for the Houston Club's well known Whiskey Pecan Cake.

At first, our baker flatly refused to reveal his secret recipe. But I finally convinced him it was for the good of the club and for his reputation as a chef of many exotic specialties.

The recipe appeared in the newspaper giving the chef full credit. Almost immediately, the columnist was besieged with letters from irate housewives. One reader described the cake as a "total disaster." "It looks like concrete," another reader wrote. She taped a sample of the icing to her letter to prove her point.

What went wrong? The baker had given us the recipe all right; but he *left out one of the main ingredients*.

Repentant, the baker agreed to send the *correct* recipe to all the upset readers who had written letters to the columnist. But he adamantly refused to have it published in the newspaper again.

You can understand why I'm reluctant to ask chefs for the secrets of their specialties. Besides, when *they* say tablespoon they refer to a huge cooking spoon.

Salad Show Biz

Making a colorful, exotic salad at the table is another form of culinary showmanship. Here are a few of the highly successful "Show Biz" salads I recommend.

Caesar Salad

(serves 4—make at table, tea cart or side table)

2 eggs
1 1/2 heads Romaine, washed
2 lemons
anchovy filets
garlic clove
grated Parmesan cheese
dry mustard, pepper mill
salt, Accent
olive oil, Worcestershire
seasoned croutons

Also, you'll need:

2 bowls, one wooden, placed in larger bowl with ice
sharp knife
salad plates (put in ice around bowl)
tablespoon
salad set (fork and spoon)
napkins
pot—boiling water and bowl
pinking shears (optional)

Coddle 2 eggs in shell in bowl of boiling water. Rub wooden salad bowl placed in ice in other bowl with garlic clove. Add 4 teaspoons olive oil in wooden bowl and rotate to spread oil. Tear romaine into bite-size pieces or cut with pinking shears. Don't bruise greens. Sprinkle over greens:

juice of 1 1/2 lemons
1/4 teaspoon dry mustard
1/4 teaspoon ground black pepper
1/2 teaspoon salt
1/4 teaspoon Accent
1/2 cup Parmesan cheese

Toss lightly but well. Break the eggs on the greens, add dash of Worcestershire and mix. Serve on chilled plates from around bowl. Top each with seasoned croutons and anchovy filet.

Chrysanthemum Salad for 4

1 pot white chrysanthemums (4 blossoms), or cut flowers may be used
dressing:
juice of 4 lemons
1 tablespoon sugar
2 tablespoons oil
mix lemon juice, sugar and oil.

Spray blossoms clean with cold water. *Be sure that all "creepy crawlers"* are removed or you will have a regrettable instead of an unforgettable show. Pluck or snip flower petals in front of your guests and place in chilled bowl. (Place small bowl in larger bowl of ice.) Pour lemon dressing slowly over petals while twirling bowl. Then toss lightly. Serve on chilled plates. Watercress petals may be mixed with chrysanthemum petals. You may make this salad in kitchen and serve for a buffet or a seated meal. It's pretty in a crystal bowl. For buffet, place lemon sugar dressing in separate serving dish. For a seated meal, mix before serving and place on a red tip lettuce leaf or crystal plate and garnish.

24-Hour Layered Green Salad

I especially like this green salad, as it can be made the day before.

Make in serving bowl, preferably the one you are going to place on the table. Layer, starting with lettuce on bottom:

chopped iceberg lettuce
sliced beets (canned and drained)
chopped fresh spinach
bean sprouts and water chestnuts, sliced
chopped green onions, fine
green peas (defrosted)
chopped cooked bacon
sliced eggs, 6–8

Top with equal parts of mayonnaise and plain yogurt. Sprinkle Parmesan cheese on top. Refrigerate for 24 hours. Serve.

Garnishes for Soups and Salads

Crumbled bacon
Chopped chives, parsley, watercress, or dill
Croutons
Grated cheese
Lemon or lime slices
Olive slices
Paprika
Whipped cream, yogurt, or sour cream
Chopped nuts
Chow mein noodles
Chrysanthemum petals
Cut outs of vegetables

Pinking shears are great to trim lettuce leaves for salad plates or buffet trays.

You can make this lovely centerpiece from watermelon baskets, with slices from the watermelon's center being used for appetizers. Votives wrapped with fresh green leaves and tied with a colorful cord enhance the centerpiece.

Centerpieces

Another way to add a touch of showmanship—economically, if you wish—is through an imaginative centerpiece. For example, on one occasion I used goldfish in brandy snifters with votive candles on a mirror in the center of the table. It's a guaranteed conversation-livener.

Attractive centerpieces can be made from just about anything—gourds, pine cones, acorns, loquat leaves and blossoms, magnolias, dried flowers, long whole cinnamon sticks, candles, floating candles, garden flowers, fresh fruits, vegetables, and desserts. Be sure to include florist tape, sticks with wires and an oasis in your planning. Even pumpkins can be made slightly sensational by painting a scene, message, or picture on them. Or, they can be used with candles inside them for an outdoor centerpiece or other decoration.

I once used African violets to good advantage for a luncheon. I had tables of 10, centered with a basket filled with 5 small pots of pink African violets. As guests left, we gave each couple a plant to bid them farewell. Don't forget to order your violets in plenty of time and specify the color. If you do have low-flowering plants, don't forget the ease and joy of using them.

Styrofoam can be cut into a ring, heart shape or a letter shape. Add fresh lettuce leaves, curly endive, parsley, fresh carved vegetable flowers with toothpicks for arrangement. (See food carvings pages 75–77.) Of course, whole fresh fruits and vegetables may be attached also. This is easy to do and easy to see over.

Centerpieces can add a delightful light touch to your party. You can make some highly "entertaining" pieces, using a little of your time and lots of imagination. For example, some unusual swan centerpieces, inspired by the Houston Club's former chef, Roberto Alaniz, and food manager, Richard Garcia, are on page 69.

Orange Tree

This centerpiece consists of orange baskets hanging from an orange tree placed on a cart or table.

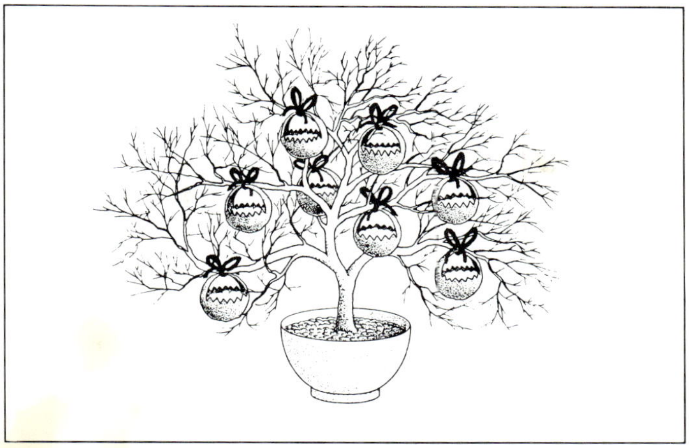

If orange baskets are to be used or served as part of a buffet, make their removal from the tree as simple as possible.

Plant a tree branch securely in fancy pot. Hang the orange baskets on branches with "twist-em" ties, pipe cleaners, or ribbons for a novel buffet centerpiece; however, use hooks (large paper clip) if baskets are to be removed.

Fill each orange basket with fruit, ambrosia, sherbet balls, tangerine yogurt or ice cream. Garnish with mint sprig and mandarin orange sections.

If orange basket is to be served, take the individual basket from tree and place on a plate containing a maple leaf or greenery and serve to your guest.

To serve from a buffet, simply let each guest remove his own basket from the tree.

For orange basket filled with sherbet or ice cream, remove from freezer 20 minutes before serving.

Ice Mold Centerpiece
(make a week ahead)

Select a plastic container that fits in your freezer. (I once used a plastic waste basket and had to remove some shelves from the freezer.) About a week before the party, fill container with about 2 inches of water, and each day add 2 or more inches of icy water, enough to cover added gadgets. For example, for a bridal shower you may daily add 2 or 3 of the following items:

Bride and groom (head first so it would be upright and at top of mold)
Thimble
Coin
Needle and thread
Garter
Artificial rosebud
Fake wedding band and diamond ring
Frying pan
Rolling pin (toy store)
Anything else traditional or 2 or 3 of each of the above items

Be sure to place items on outer edge so they are visible when unmolded.

For other occasions: Horsey set—miniature horses or gilded horse shoes; bon voyage—miniature ships; bankers—coins, miniature savings banks.

Unmold into a drip pan and trim with ivy or greenery to hide pan.

Ice Mold

The day before it is needed, prepare a large, shallow roasting pan by spraying it with vegetable oil. Fill with cold water, and freeze overnight.

To remove: invert into a shallow aluminum pan a little longer than the ice. Place hot, damp towel over bottom of pan, and shake to release ice. Keep frozen until serving time.

To keep ice level, put crushed foil underneath block. Arrange food (shrimp, relishes, strawberries, etc.) on top. This can be made in any shape.

That Personal Touch

Centerpieces

Desert Theme—Seated Dinner
(for each 60-inch table of 8)

8 individual cacti in 2- to 3-inch square pots
1/2 gallon white sand or fine gravel
small charcoal chips or redwood chips
brown wrapping paper
yellow yarn
felt-tip pen
foil or cardboard circle

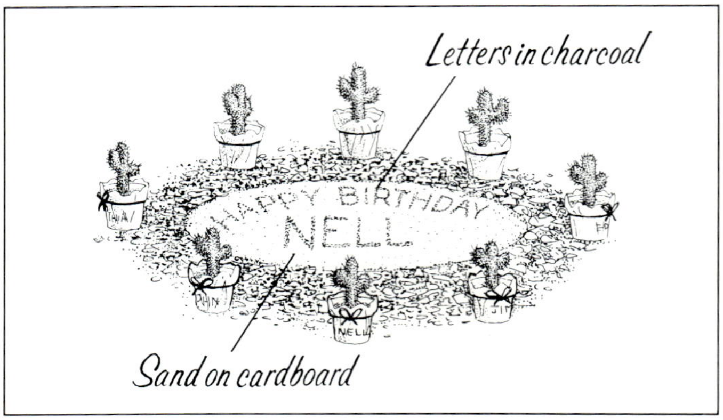

This is an example of a centerpiece with a desert theme.

Wrap individual pots with brown paper, tie with yarn and write guest's name on each pot. Cover center of table with foil or cardboard circle. Cover circle with sand or gravel. Place pots of cacti on edge of sand, one in front of each guest. Write with charcoal or redwood chips the name of the honoree or message (Happy Birthday) on sand in center of table. Outline centerpiece to include pots with charcoal or redwood chips.

Cacti are souvenirs for guests.

An acorn squash with a lid can hold many surprises!

Acorn Squash

Here's an idea for a personal touch decoration we used on our acorn squash lid. The squash was filled with chicken martinique, (see recipe page 67). Cranberries popped out at you when lifting the elephant-studded lid. They were inserted in the squash half, around the edge. (See pumpkin soup recipe, page 81.)

Food Ideas

Messages that accompany food are a delightful way to add a personal touch. The following are some ideas guaranteed to make your guests feel welcome and special.

Special Attention for Guests

melon, grapefruit half, pineapple basket
2 toothpicks
1 small card (placecard size)
ribbon
fine wire
flower, or small bow

Place toothpicks 1 inch apart on one side of melon, grapefruit half, or pineapple basket.

Write message on card (Welcome Jean, or Bon Voyage) and put hole in each end of card.

Attach card to toothpicks with ribbon or fine wire by threading through holes at each end of card. Tie bow or wire fresh flower on front of card around ribbon.

Christmas Newlyweds

Use small Christmas tree with cake slice for December party. I added white hard sauce on fruit cake and decorated with red icing initials of bride and groom and a heart for a December newlywed couple.

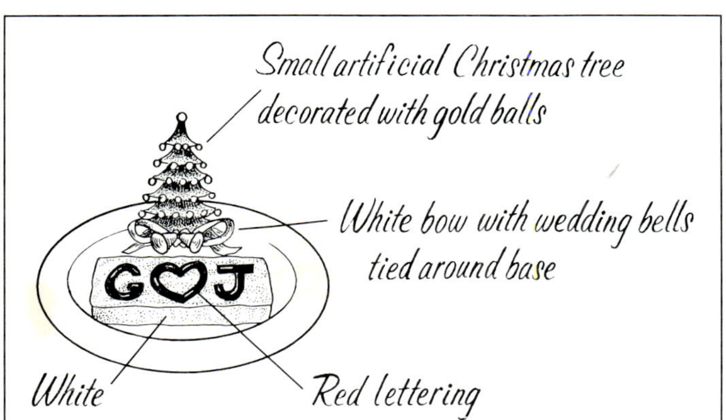

"Baseball Boy"

The following is what I did for a surprise party I had for Eddie, and you might do it for your favorite "sport." Buy individual gingerbread cookie. (They are available in different sizes and shapes at bakeries.) Put on cookie tray for

centerpiece. Write name and make hat with tube icing. Add baseball bat made out of paper. Stick cookie on oasis on tray and cover with flowers. For a college roommate, Barbara Longmire's visit, I used a "girl cookie," and wrote "Welcome Roomie."

Food Artistry—Carving and Decorating

Still another way to add flair to your table is through food-carving and decorating.

Flower-carving is one of the most popular of all carvings. Make your flowers to suit the occasion and season. And be sure to practice first on simple flowers.

Suitable vegetables for carving are white turnips, potatoes, cucumbers, yellow and zucchini squash, rutabagas, red beets, and carrots. Or, you can soak turnips or potatoes in food coloring or Easter egg dye, to change the color.

Food coloring or watercolor paint may be used. It should be applied with a small brush and *not* overdone. Colored carvings should be kept away from water, because they will fade. The carved vegetables may be kept fresh in water in the refrigerator for repeated use.

Tools for simple food carving include:

1. Small paring knife
2. Melon ball scoop for cutting round balls of vegetables or fruit
3. Potato peeler
4. Scissors—plain and pinking shears
5. Crinkle or waffle cutter (best are from restaurant supply house)
6. Pastry bag and tube

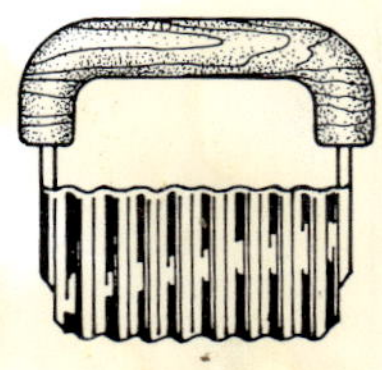

Clever and decorative additions to food can be made from potatoes, turnips, carrots, beets, or sheet pans of firm gelatin, pie dough, cake, bread, or cookie dough.

Vegetables

Example: with a potato:

Slice into desired thickness,

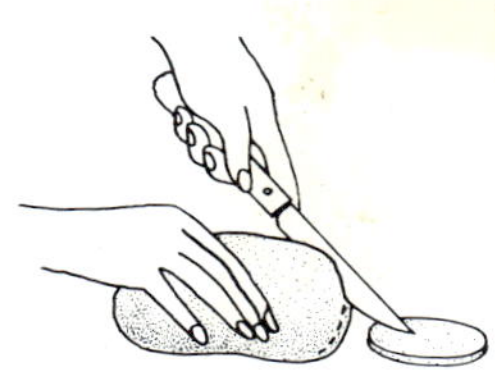

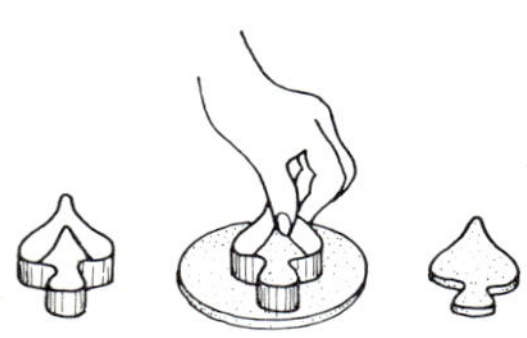

or cut your own pattern from freezer paper or wax paper. (A child's coloring book is an excellent source.) Place your pattern on the vegetable slice, secure with toothpicks if necessary.

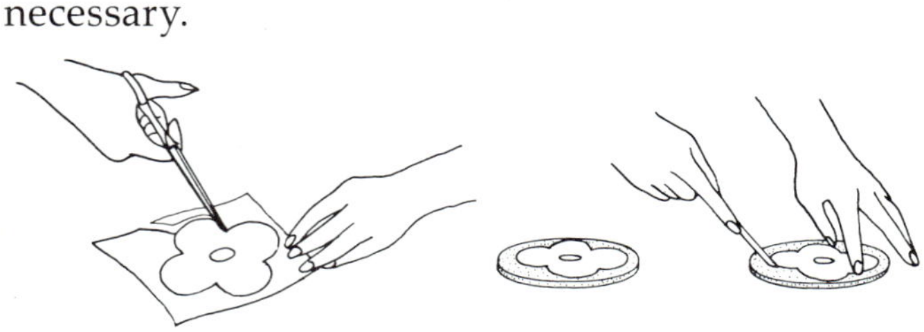

Trim with sharp knife or vegetable shears. Numbers and letters may be made in the same manner.

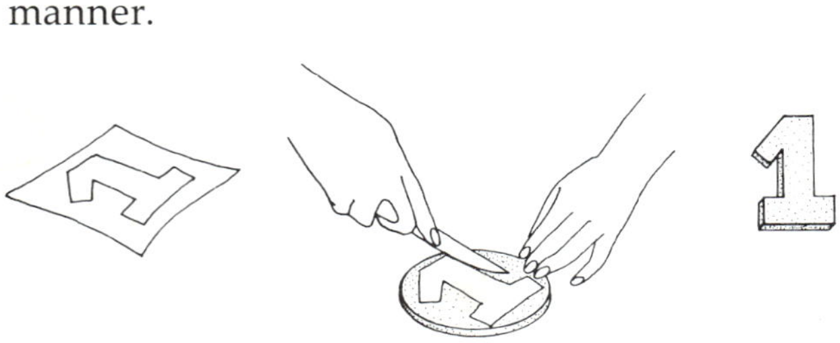

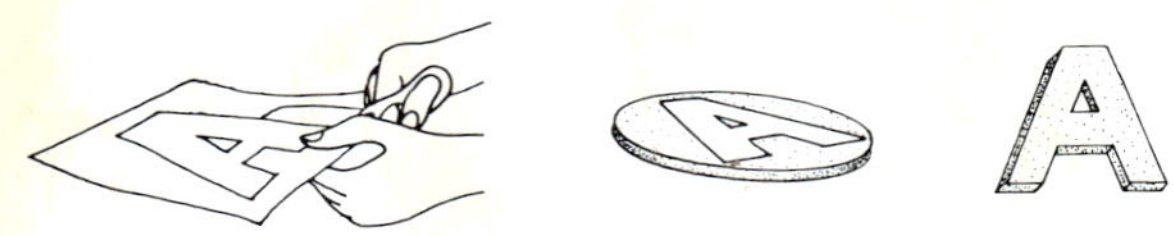

Dimension may be added by scooping areas out with small spoon or scoop.

Radish flowers or squash (see "Posh Squash" page 68)—slice petals on all sides without cutting petal off. These may be placed on toothpicks or used directly on relish and hors d'oeuvre trays.

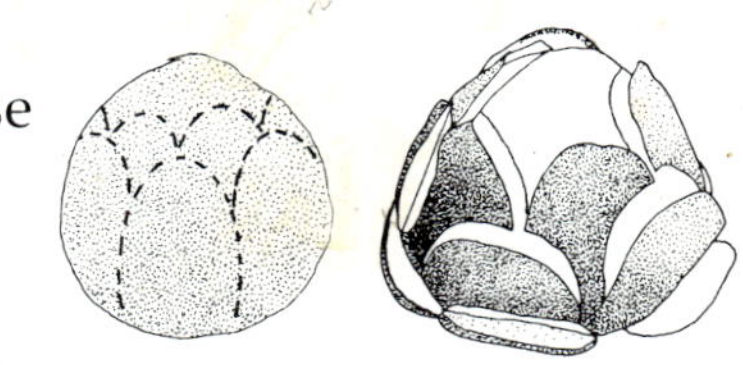

Tomato or orange roses—with sharp knife, peel fruit in one continuous row approximately 1/4 to 1/2 inch in width. Make strip as thin as possible but thick enough not to break. Reverse strip and recoil. The "flower" should rest on flat slice at the end.

For arrangements of flowers, the vegetable flowers may be put on wire stems —

Flat arrangements:
use parsley for greenery—

Fruit

Baskets—oranges, lemons, grapefruit, melons, pineapple. These have endless possibilities. They can be filled and used to serve a variety of relishes, desserts, salads, vegetables, flambé items, or for centerpieces.

Example: orange basket
Draw outline on fruit—

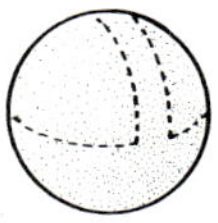

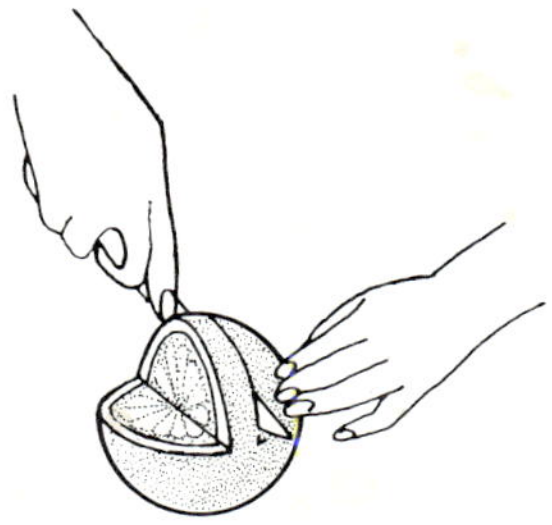

Cut top sections from basket—

Hollow basket—
Edges may be trimmed
with pinking shears—

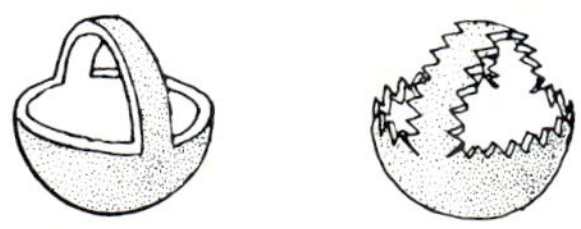

Melons—

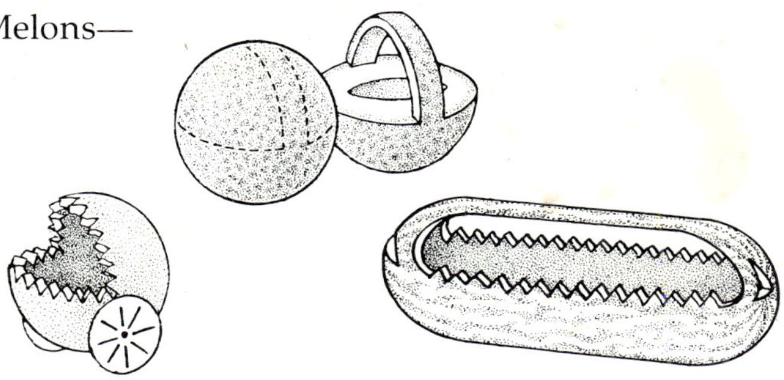

Pineapple—
Pineapple may be cut lengthwise. Hollow and

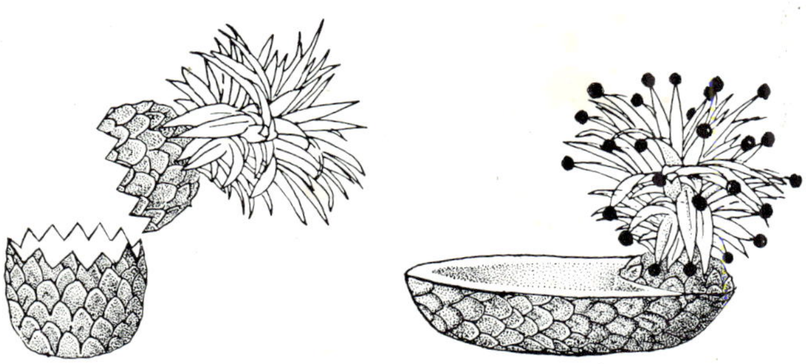

fill. Use greenery top for decoration. Cranberries can be placed on it for color.

Fruit Gelatin Slices

Use orange, grapefruit, lemon, lime, apple or melon cut in half; scoop out and fill with flavored gelatin. Reduce by one fourth the amount of water in making gelatin. Let chill and when molded, cut slices of wedges for decorating or added touch. Children love them.

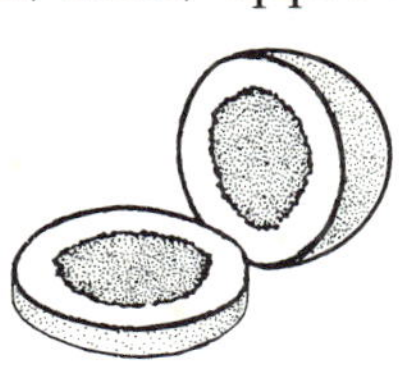

Red . . . Red . . . Red!

As I mentioned in Chapter 1, I've always loved the color red, and this infatuation has led me to use it as often as possible in foods and garnishes.

Ideas for Red Food Color Garnished for Maximum Color Attractiveness

Accompaniments
Apple jelly
Berry-apple sauce
Cherry jelly
Cranberry glace, jelly and relish
Currant jelly
Gelatin, diced or cubed
Loganberry jelly
Raspberry jelly
Wine jelly

Fruits
Candied apples, whole, rings, wedges
Cherries, whole, chopped, candied, fresh
Cranberries
Grapes, frosted, plain, whole, sliced, halved
Maraschino cherries
Pomegranate seeds
Red raspberries
Strawberries
Watermelon cubes, balls
Crab apples
Red pears

Vegetables
Beets, pickled, relish, roses
Cherry tomatoes
Pimento, chopped, strips, cut in party shapes
Red cabbage
Red peppers, rings, strips, shredded
Radishes, sliced, roses, grated
Tomatoes, aspic, catsup

Miscellaneous
Cinnamon drops
Crushed peppermint candy or canes
Paprika
Red bordered or pretty colorful dishes

Chapter Five

How to Create "Fun Beginnings" for Your Parties

First impressions are always important. The appetizers, or first course, and hors d'oeuvres you serve before the regular meal should be especially tasty and eye-appealing. They set the pace for a special party.

When individual servings are prepared, it's important that they be carefully done—and beautiful. *Remember, each guest sees only his individual serving!*

For seated luncheons or dinners of more than 6 planned at home, or at a hotel or restaurant, it is generally better to avoid hot first courses. Keeping production in the kitchen simple generally ensures the quality and punctuality of the main course.

Guests are not usually served on the planned time schedule because of one circumstance or another. A *hot* soup course is one dish to absolutely avoid unless it's for a small party and you have ample help. For the latter, I offer you an ideal pumpkin soup recipe (page 81), presented in an acorn squash, which helps to keep the soup hot.

For large parties a hot first course increases the risk of lesser quality. It's not worth it! A well garnished and special cold first course is best.

Combining the appetizer with the salad for a first course saves time, labor, and dishes. You may eliminate one of these courses, especially if you've served hors d'oeuvres or food during the reception. This speeds up service and ensures better overall food quality and service.

There is no hors d'oeuvre you can't make larger or add in number for a first course. Nor is there any first course or appetizer you can't "adjust" for your hors d'oeuvre table. For example, here is a unique hors d'oeuvre I often serve in the living room during a reception. It is a large fish made of caviar and salmon for each guest to indulge himself. (See Salmon-Caviar Fish recipe, below.) This can also be served at dinner as a first course. (See Individual Smoked Salmon Appetizer recipe, page 80.)

Cold Hors d'Oeuvres

Salmon-Caviar Fish

cream cheese (Tabasco, lemon juice, onion juice)
smoked salmon (cut into bite sizes)
black caviar
finely chopped egg white
finely chopped egg yolk
sour cream
capers for salmon
finely chopped parsley
small party rye bread sliced and rice crackers

Mix cream cheese, Tabasco, lemon and onion juice together. On large tray, mold mixed spread in fish shape—

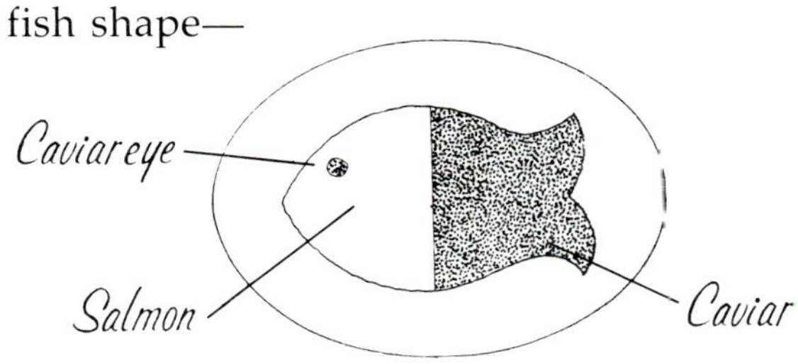

Cover front half of fish shape with smoked salmon and the back half with black caviar—

Neatly decorate smoked salmon with capers. Use caviar for eye of fish. Outline caviar on back half of fish with three lines starting with chopped egg whites. Then egg yolk and finally the sour cream—

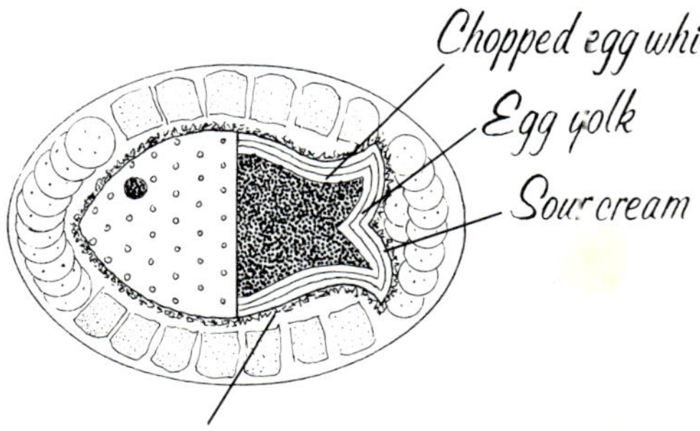

Outline bottom of fish with finely chopped parsley

Surround the entire fish with small bread slices and crackers.

For Salmon-Caviar Fish appetizer, duplicate this recipe on individual plate using only enough cream cheese to make serving 1/4 inch thick.

Note: Excellent domestic caviar may be purchased at a much lower price than the expensive imported. I doubt that anyone can distinguish between the two, unless they bring their microscope.

Patés and Spreads

Paté for buffet, hors d'oeuvres, or appetizers, is a delectable and impressive way to use leftover, well-cooked meat: smoked turkey, ham, beef, veal, chicken liver, cheese, or fish.

2 cups cooked diced meat
1 8-ounce package cream cheese, cut into pieces

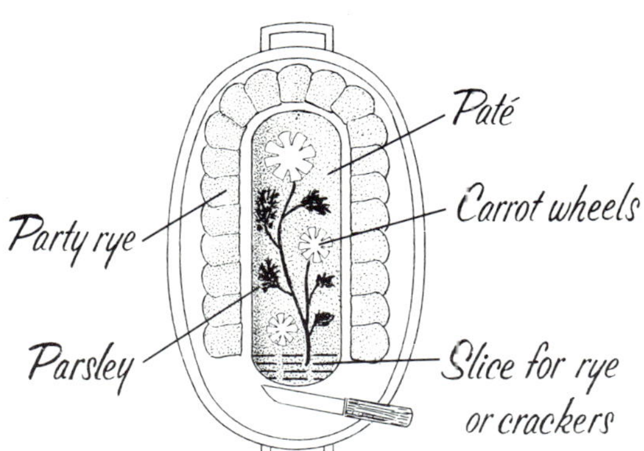

Mold paté to fit bread or crackers

Prepare meat in blender or food processor until smooth. Add cream cheese gradually. Season as you wish. Perhaps: 1/4 raw onion, 1 tablespoon lemon juice, dash salt, cracked pepper, pinch of cinnamon or ground cloves.

Paté may be foil-wrapped in long loaves to fit small crackers or party rye, and frozen for up to six months. When guests drop in, defrost in microwave or oven, place on serving dish, decorate, and place crackers around or near with knife to serve. May also be served hot on thin sliced toast, French bread, pumpernickel slices or other bread of your choice.

Canapés are difficult to make and still harder to maintain at a high quality level. Patés and spreads are preferable. Recently, I used my smoked turkey paté from the freezer for a Christmas party. We had just enough to shape 3 small Christmas trees on a tray and garnish with tiny kumquat Christmas tree balls, and a

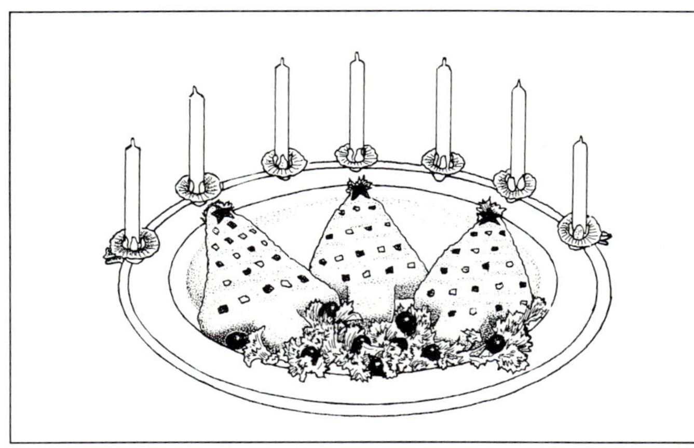

pimento star at the top. One side of the tray was decorated with clip-on candle holders filled with red candles. Whole cranberries and parsley sprigs trimmed the other side of the tray, which was placed toward the guests on the table.

Individual Acorn Squash Filled with Pumpkin Soup with Whole Fresh Cranberries

Buy small, individually selected, well-shaped acorn squash with stem on top. With sharp knife make a very thin slice off the bottom of the squash so it will sit flat. Slice the top off the squash approximately 1/4-inch below the stem and save this portion for a "lid." Scoop out

Create your wonderful "fun beginning" by featuring a watermelon slice topped with half a choyote squash filled with crabmeat and shrimp, and garnished with melon balls, celery leaves, and capers.

center. For soup, use your favorite vichyssoise recipe, substituting fresh pumpkin for potatoes (or see following recipe).

Slightly bake acorn squash (20 minutes) just enough that it does not have a raw appearance. With melon-ball scoop, make 4 or 5 holes around edge of squash to place whole raw cranberries for extra flair. When ready to serve, heat pumpkin soup very hot, pour in acorn squash, and place in oven to ensure both are hot. With "lid" off squash add Parmesan cheese and very finely chopped parsley. Then, serve immediately with lid on for guests to remove. (May be made a couple of days ahead of time.)

Pumpkin Soup

1 can pumpkin pie filling
1 can milk

Mix in saucepan and heat. Pour in squash, hot. We used this acorn squash idea for a dinner honoring Republican ladies. It was filled with a Chicken Martinique and adorned with a brightly painted dancing elephant holding a welcome sign. A toothpick was taped to the back of the elephant and stuck in the squash lid (see page 74).

Crisis: One evening when Marianne and Roger Staubach were dining with us, I chose this specialty to begin our meal. I noted that Roger got his soup spoon stuck in the squash. Be sure to use small soup spoons.

Apple with Seafood First Lady
(4 to 6 portions)

1 lb king crabmeat cut in chunks
12 cooked shrimp
4 chopped shallots
3 tablespoons butter
1/3 cup dry sherry
salt and pepper to taste
1 3/4 cups heavy cream (optional)
3 tablespoons flour (optional)
1 clove garlic, finely chopped
2 tablespoons brandy, to burn off

Melt butter in saucepan. Add shallots and garlic, and continue cooking for a minute or so. Then, add the flour and cook for 2 more minutes; add the cream and cook for 5 more minutes. Sauté crabmeat and shrimp in butter and add brandy. Burn off brandy by igniting it. Then, add shrimp and crabmeat to sauce and heat. Last, add sherry and remove from heat and serve.

Core a large apple and soak in white wine. Bake and continue to add white wine as needed. Serve apple with crabmeat and shrimp added to it and place on a bed of rice if you like. A whole fresh artichoke may be used in place of apple.

Planning a Cocktail Party

If you're having a cocktail party with hors d'oeuvres from six to eight in the evening, have plenty of food on hand because your guests will make *this* their dinner. Plan a certain number of each item per guest. Increase the number of items if the party is at the dinner hour, if there are men at the party, or if the party promises to last longer than two hours.

Obviously, the greater variety of appetizers you serve, the fewer you'll have to prepare for each individual delicacy. Just make sure you have plenty of the most *popular* items on hand. And while you're at it, plan to have some easy replacements in case you do run out of food. Good planning will preclude most of this type of emergency. But when that embarrassing moment does occur, I like to use these emergency refills: cheese—spreads or easy-to-cut varieties; items in jars or cans, such as olives, mushroom caps, artichoke hearts, pickled cauliflower, shrimp, patés, pickled corn, quail eggs, caviar or smoked oysters.

Again, I can't overemphasize the need to make your hors d'oeuvre trays beautiful—and different! Here are some tips for making these trays esthetically pleasing:

* Use attractive, unusual containers, trays, mirrors, platters or baskets.
* Be certain the total look is well coordinated as to color, shape, and balance.
* For tray decorations, use small dolls, Christmas trees, Easter bunnies, ice molds, squash swan, fresh flowers, bows, food flowers made from beets, radishes, and colored turnips; top of pineapple decorated with whole cranberries, flags, lemon or orange flowers or baskets, or food flowers.
* Avoid the picket-fence look! Have toothpicks, if needed, in a small container. Provide a receptacle for used toothpicks or shrimp tails. It is *perfectly correct* and often more comfortable to use one's fingers.
* Have plenty of napkins and plates for drippy foods; have proper utensils with which to serve.
* In addition to the main table or buffet, it is well to spread out one's goodies over smaller tables, which should be placed where guests are likely to congregate. By all means, try to avoid a jam around the main table. For example, you might elect to set up a cheese-and-fruit table, a chafing-dish table; and a sweets table—all of course in strategic locations. Don't forget to put napkins on each small table.
* Underliners or tray trimmings can include greenery from your yard or garden, such as

holly, tree leaves, pine, mint, parsley, lettuce, spinach, romaine, curly endive, purple cabbage or carrots shredded or chopped fine and sprinkled in a pattern, hard gelatin (colored) a pond or diced, flowers made of tomatoes, squash, celery, lemons, grapefruit, potatoes, or white onions.

* You can glaze hors d'oeuvres and appetizers for a professional effect (see page 84).

Special tools should include pinking shears, which are great for trimming romaine, or other greenery, and for trimming oranges or lemon baskets/cups.

Other tools include waffle cutter; wastebasket or container for ice mold; molds, cake bundt pan; melon-ball cutter; sharp-pointed paring knife; grapefruit knife; peeler; knife sharpener (cut away from you, using cutting board); pastry bag.

I'm including some of my all-star list of hors d'oeuvre and buffet selections to save your having to thumb through scores of cookbooks, magazines, and recipe files in quest of that "perfect dish." Many of these selections were adapted from recipes used at world-famous restaurants and hotels. Others are my own. Preparation time varies. Some of the servings require considerable time and effort. Others can be done quickly and easily. Whatever your choice, be sure to maintain overall *quality and appearance.* To get you started here is a sample hors d'oeuvre menu. (Also see page 92 for cheese.)

Hot and Cold Items for 25 Guests (men and women).

Time: 6 to 8 p.m.

Hot—	Quiche Lorraine	2 1-inch squares per person
	Dates stuffed with pecans and bacon chips or wrapped in bacon. (Make day before and refrigerate. Heat in 300° oven until bacon is crisp. Serve immediately.)	2 per person
Cold—	Iced shrimp, red sauce	6 medium per person
	Assorted fancy hors d'oeuvres and relishes	3 per person
	Petite ham slices, orange nut bread tiny rolls	2 per person
	Total	15 per person

Dainties for Your Hors d'oeuvre or Buffet Table

Put these with desserts and sweets and serve at the end of your food line.

Fresh Fruit
Kiwi, black cherries with stems, fresh seedless grapes.
Strawberries filled with crème de menthe whipped cream.
Kumquat filled with cranberry relish.
Miniature avocados (need to be ordered in advance from your grocer.)

Dried Fruit
Dates, stuffed with nuts, apricots, pineapple.
Yogurt-covered raisins.

Canned Fruit
Mandarin oranges, pitted bing cherries, seedless grapes.
Pineapple chunks, packed in water. Fruit gelatin slices, page 77.

Sweets
Miniature pastries or cookies.
Pralines
Turtles
Mints
Nuts

Glaze for Fancy Appetizers or Hors d'oeuvres

This glaze can give a truly professional touch to baked ham/turkey or a paté. Soak 1½

You can make your fancy hors d'oeuvres and centerpieces (in this case pineapple/zucchini turkey) look even more elegant by placing them on a mirror.

tablespoons plain gelatin in 2 tablespoons cold water. Place mixture in bowl and add 1/2 cup boiling water. Cool to room temperature. Spoon over hors d'oeuvres on cake rack with pan under to catch excess.

Note: Leftover gelatin may be refrigerated and used again. To reduce to liquid state, place in a pan of hot water. The same procedure may be used for glaze by using melted tomato madrilene. For added flavor, use chilled wine in place of cold water.

Baked Ham/Turkey or Paté á la Professional Chefs (Chaud-Froid)

1 package (1 tablespoon) powdered gelatin
1/2 cup white wine, chicken bouillon, or water
1/2 cup mayonnaise
1/2 cup sour cream
food coloring, if desired

Dissolve gelatin in wine or other liquid. Let stand 5 minutes to soften. Dissolve over simmering water (double boiler) for 10 to 15 minutes. Remove, and stir mayonnaise and sour cream into the mixture. Add food coloring if desired. Place 15 minutes in freezer by timer until semi-set.

For ham/turkey—trim cold ham/turkey until smooth and place on cake rack. Pour mixture over ham/turkey and spread.

For paté—using a spatula, frost outside. Return to refrigerator for 30 minutes longer (or 5 minutes by timer in freezer). Decorate with spiced pineapple ring for ham, fresh green grapes, watercress, or slices of kumquats, mandarin oranges or see "Food Artistry" in Chapter 4 for carved-food decorations.

Assorted Fancy Hors d'oeuvres and Relishes

Select 4 to 6 of these items per tray: fresh raw vegetables, cut into easy-to-eat sizes with a waffle cutter, can give this item a distinctive look and permit a variety of shapes. (See page 76.) Cut a slice off the bottom of cherry tomatoes and rosebud beets to ensure they will stand and not roll on the tray. You may use fresh cauliflower, broccoli, small asparagus spears, snow peas, carrots, mushrooms, whole fresh artichokes, and jicama. Use yellow or zucchini squash crown half-filled with cheese and topped with cauliflower or broccoli flower. Beware! Dips are drippy and difficult to eat. Cheese balls or logs are easy to make and can be a good alternative. (See page 92.)

Beets, zucchini, yellow squash, mushrooms, cherry tomatoes, rosebud beets, small brussel sprouts, cucumbers, potatoes, radishes and hard-cooked eggs may be filled with a seafood salad, chicken or shrimp, paté, crabmeat, cream or cottage cheese, cheddar cheese spread, caviar, ham spread, and guacamole. Or, you can make your own paté.

Stuffed Cherry Tomatoes

1 pint cherry tomatoes (about 22)
1/2 lb cheddar cheese, finely grated
2 or 3 tablespoons mayonnaise
1 teaspoon Dijon mustard
dash of cayenne pepper

Cut slice about 1/3 from top of each tomato. With a small, sharp knife, hollow out the pulp. Remove a very thin slice from the bottom of each tomato to sit flat on serving plate. Combine remaining ingredients in food processor. Blend just until smooth. Using pastry bag with star-shaped tip, pipe mixture into tomatoes or use a sharp pointed teaspoon to fill. Chill until serving time.

Cherry Tomatoes with Crabmeat

Prepare tomatoes same as in above recipe and fill with crabmeat salad, tuna, caviar, salmon, or egg salad.

Marinated Shrimp

10 lbs shrimp (peeled and cooked)
3 cups oil
1/2 gallon dry white wine
3/4 gallon white vinegar
6 medium purple onions, very finely chopped
4 tablespoons celery seed (whole)
Tabasco sauce to flavor
1/2 cup finely chopped parsley
1 cup capers

Mix all ingredients together and let stand for 1 hour at least. Then add shrimp to marinade and let stand for 24 hours in the refrigerator.

Artichoke Bottoms with Shrimp Paté
(for 8 to 10 shells)

Drain peeled canned artichoke shells. Put in blender 3/4 cup diced, peeled, drained, cooked shrimp; 2 tablespoons lime juice; 1 whole plum cut into slivers; 1/2 teaspoon curry; and 1/4 cup mayonnaise. Blend until a paste consistency. Remove from blender and with spoon or very small scoop fill shells. Garnish with sliver of plum or dot of pimento. (See other paté recipes pages 80 and 84.)

Tiny Tart Shells for Hors d'oeuvres, Vegetables or Desserts

3 cups flour, sifted
1 1/2 teaspoons salt
1 cup shortening
1 tablespoon butter
6 tablespoons milk, cold

Resift flour with salt. Cut in shortening and butter. Add liquid, mixing just until dough holds together; round up in a ball. Roll thin and line 36 (3-by-1 inch) tart pans. Prick with fork. Bake in very hot oven (475°) until rich, golden brown, about 8 minutes. Cool before filling. Place on a lovely tiered plate or gleaming silver tray. For added flair, each little pastry may be garnished. Pie crust mix or cookie mix may be used for shells.

Simple Pastry Cream for Tarts
(makes 1 2/3 cups)

1 package (3 5/8-ounce) instant vanilla pudding-and-pie filling mix
1 1/2 cups light cream
1/4 teaspoon almond extract or 1/2 teaspoon praline paste

Make pudding mix as package label directs, substituting 1 1/2 cups light cream for the milk and adding the almond extract.

Refrigerate, covered, until ready to use.

Fill tart shells with pastry cream.

Topping for Tarts

Seedless green grapes, fresh berries, mandarin oranges, or bananas.

Glazes for Tarts

Apricot—heat 1/2 cup apricot jam over medium heat. Add 2 tablespoons sugar and 1 tablespoon lemon juice and cook until sugar is dissolved. Strain the mixture and cool. (Optional: add 2 tablespoons apricot liqueur.) While glaze is slightly warm, spoon over cooled tart.

Currant—heat 1/2 cup currant jelly with 2 tablespoons Framberry (raspberry brandy). Stir until jelly is melted. This is especially good over strawberry or blueberry tarts.

Hot Hors d'oeuvres

* Quiche Lorraine or pizza, make on cookie sheet. When ready to serve, cut in 1-inch squares before removing from pans.

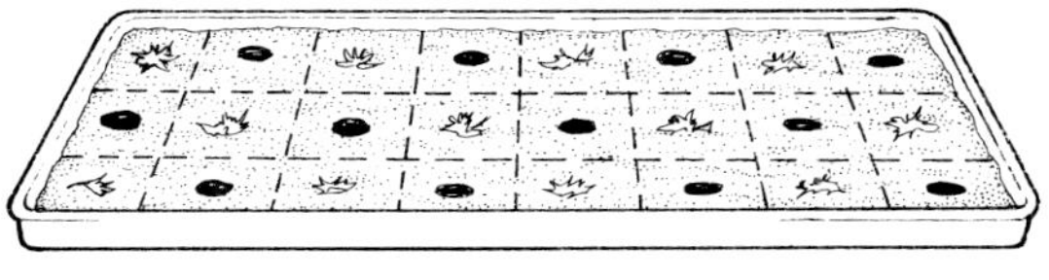

* Petite hamburgers, some with cheese. These can be fun, substantial, and relished.
* Fried boneless turkey pieces (bite size).
* Cocktail franks—heat in a mixture of equal parts of currant jelly and yellow prepared mustard.

* Egg rolls with sweet-sour and mustard sauces.
* Stuffed mushrooms, or zucchini crowns—see following recipe.
* Gourmet oysters—see following recipe.
* Puffs or balls made of cheese, chicken, sausage, ham, crabmeat, sauerkraut, broccoli.
* Cold or hot ham or smoked turkey slices with cheese biscuits, orange nut bread. (Be sure meat fits bread size.)
* Bacon-wrapped pineapple, olives, dates, scallops, chicken livers, franks and water chestnuts.
* Melba toast rounds with deviled ham with chutney, anchovy fillets, petite shrimp on cheese, crab mixed with capers and buttered crumbs, smoked pork tenderloin slices with mustard.
* Suggested items for marinade—shrimp, turkey fingers, ham squares, lobster, chicken livers, beef cubes. Have toothpicks for serving.

Quick and Simple Marinade for Hors d'oeuvres

1/4 cup oil
1 cup wine
1/2 cup Escoffier sauce
1/4 cup vinegar

Or marinade in your favorite Italian-type dressing for approximately 2 hours before broiling to brown and then bake till done.

Stuffed Zucchini Crowns
(for crowns, see page 69)

1 package (10 ounces) frozen chopped spinach
1 egg
1/3 cup all bran crumbs
2 tablespoons Parmesan cheese
2 tablespoons sunflower seeds
salt, pepper, nutmeg to taste
3 zucchini, approximately 1 1/4 inches in diameter and 6 1/2 inches long

Place frozen block of spinach in small, heavy pot. Cook over moderate heat until you can break apart in pieces; cover and cook until hot throughout, about 3 minutes. Drain excess liquid. Combine spinach in bowl with egg, crumbs, cheese, seeds, and seasonings. Wash zucchini; cut off 1/2-inch slice at each end. Cut into pieces 1 inch long. Scoop most of pulp from each piece, leaving shell with thin base. Blanch shells in boiling water until slightly tender, 2 or 3 minutes. Mound filling in hollow of each shell and arrange shells on baking sheet. Bake in pre-heated 375° oven for 5 minutes. Serve immediately or at room temperature. Makes about 15.

London Beef Roll

This is perfect for a cocktail buffet. It is an excellent substitute for beef tenderloin and much less expensive. This recipe makes 8 small slices.

very sharp knife
1 flank steak (1 1/2-pound to 2-pound flank)

Split flank lengthwise, butterfly style and fill with meat stuffing. Roll, similar to jelly roll. Bake

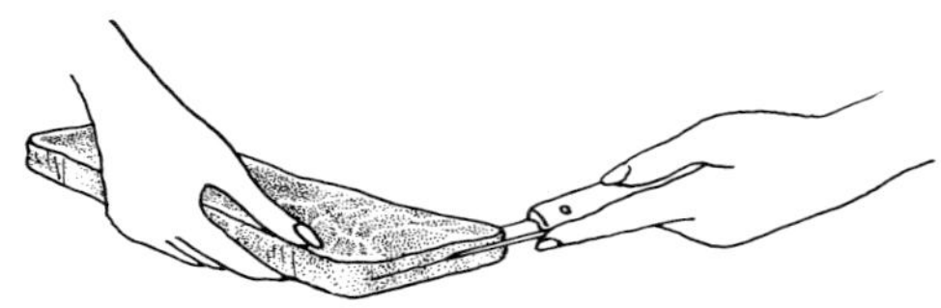

Split flank

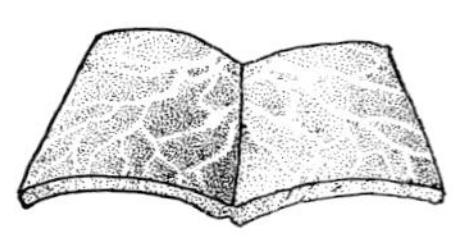

Open

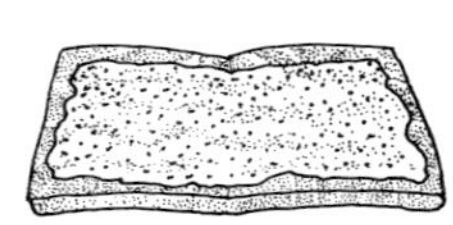

Fill

Roll

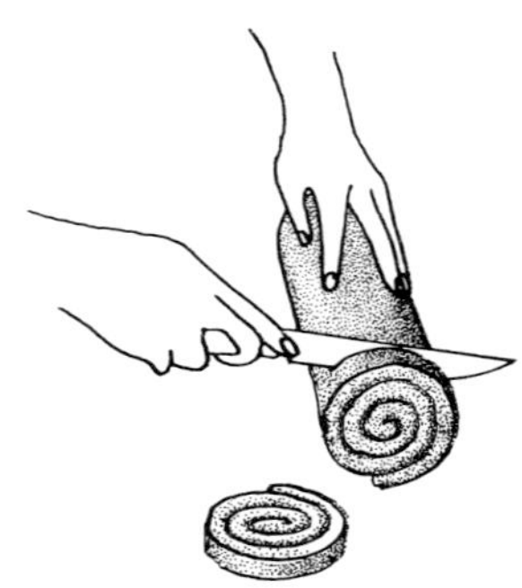

Bake and slice

in oven 350° for about 35 minutes. Slice thin and serve on small rolls or as a main dish.

Meat Stuffing

(also for yellow squash or lamb chops)

Mix together and brown mixture in skillet and use for stuffing:

1 pound raw hamburger meat
1 egg
1/2 cup red wine
1/4 cup tomato juice
salt, white pepper, and dash powdered fennel (spice)

Gourmet Oysters

(serves 8)

1/4 pound butter
2 cups onion, finely chopped
1/2 pint heavy cream
1 quart oysters
2 1/2 ounces red wine or bourbon
salt and pepper to taste

Wash oysters and drain. Melt butter in skillet; do not brown. Add onions and saute until clear. Add cream; bring to boil. Add oysters, seasoning, and bourbon. Heat quickly until oysters are set and begin to curl. Serve oysters in chafing dish. Have toothpicks nearby.

Chapter Six

How to Select and Serve Spirits

The pre-dinner social period has become a universal gesture of hospitality. Having a "glass in hand" should be a pleasurable experience for your guests. The reception hour should help to create a mood of relaxation and set the stage for a successful party or meeting.

You should normally serve a choice of drinks—including non-alcoholic beverages—unless you want to select a specific beverage such as wine or spiced tea for the occasion. In any case, you should be *prepared* to handle requests for water, juices, and soda drinks.

I always limit my pre-dinner cocktail sessions to 1 hour. This applies to parties at home and away. The relatively limited cocktail party tends to curb overindulgence and "starvation," which most guests appreciate. As a result, I instruct bartenders to measure liquor carefully, allowing 1 to 1½ ounces per drink. If guests request more, as they often do, we comply with their wishes. Wine should be poured only half way, or slightly below, in the glass. This modest approach maintains reasonable consumption, reduces waste, and allows the wine to "breathe."

Do you have to be a connoisseur of wines to stage a successful party? Definitely not. You will be able to serve any type beverage graciously—and quite confidently—by mastering the material in this chapter.

What type wine should you serve at your dinner—red, white, or rosé? Many agonize endlessly over this question when serving wine at a party, or when ordering wine with their meal in a restaurant. Their concern generally is that they might be making a social blunder or in some way violating protocol by serving or ordering the "wrong" wine.

My advice is to relax; the choice is entirely yours. You won't be "wrong," whatever selection you make. It's what you like that counts. Even for the wine experts or the more refined "sniffer and sipper"—one should enjoy the wine of his choice. I did not arrive at this conclusion frivolously. I reached this decision many years ago after a study of the major distinctions between red and white wines.

There are robust, dry red wines; there are robust, dry white wines, with varying degrees of sweetness. Frankly, if you close your eyes and sip both, it's a challenge at times to tell the difference. So, be confident, *be yourself,* be independent—and be *happy!* Order white wine or red wine, sweet or dry, sparkling or still. You'll be "right," whatever you do.

Actually, wines fall into five major categories, and flavors vary from very sweet to very dry, from American to imported. Wines generally contain 12 to 14 percent alcohol. They are usually listed in this order on menus:

1. White wines (Chablis, Rhine wine, Sauterne, Burgundy white)
2. Red wines (Burgundy, claret, Bordeaux, Chianti)
3. Rosé wines (Loire, Portugal, California)
4. Sparkling wines (champagne, sparkling Burgundy)
5. Appetizers and dessert wines (sherry, port, muscatel, vermouth, fortified wines) 20 percent alcohol

It is simple to identify a wine by the shape of its bottle.

Incidentally, when dining out it's preferable to order wines by *number.* Waiters, or the wine steward (sommelier), get bottles from the bins or storage by number. Very often, they can't pronounce the names any better than some of us can.

A quick glance at the bottle can tell you if it's a Bordeaux or Burgundy, Moselle (green) or Rhine (brown).

Very sweet wines are generally enjoyed with desserts or at an afternoon tea party. However, if you like the sweet flavor, drink it with your steak or whatever you like. Dry wines have less sugar.

American wine does not suffer in quality because it is domestic. It must be judged on its own merit. It's a matter of personal choice. Compare and make your own judgment, but do not rule out wine you like simply because it is "domestic."

America does indeed produce some excellent wines. And more and more they are receiving world-wide acclaim and acceptance. The growth of the wine industry in California, New York, and Michigan has been amazing. Wine making is also increasing in Washington, Oregon, Ohio, Illinois, Indiana, and Texas. People in these states have joined the industry not only as a hobby, but as a viable business. There's another advantage in using local wines—you save import taxes and transportation costs.

Occasions may arise when you want to present rare bottles of wholly extraordinary quality wine to fellow wine enthusiasts. I suggest you go to your nearest wine dealer and let him advise you on what to give. Or, perhaps you can call the restaurant manager ahead of time and enlist his help. Incidentally, price is not always the determining factor in making such a decision.

There are several factors to consider in the care and serving of wine. For one thing, wine is highly perishable. It should be stored in a dark, cool place, and on its side so that the wine rests against the cork. If the cork dries out and the air gets in, alas, the wine will turn to vinegar. The wines that don't turn to vinegar after they have been opened several days are fortified wines such as sherry or port.

The romantic and sophisticated sherries and ports are of a higher alcohol content than other wines. Both are blended, still (not sparkling) wines fortified with brandy to be about 20 percent alcohol. Again, most wines are 12 to 14 percent alcohol.

The saying that all wines improve with age is a myth. Most red wines do, but many white wines reach their prime in 2 to 6 years. Wines that do age in the bottle have a sediment and should be handled carefully before serving. Never shake the bottle.

Open and decant older wines, which have started to crust the bottle, several hours before serving. Serve red wines at room temperature (68°) or slightly chilled, fortified wines (sherries, and others with higher alcohol content) at room temperature (though some sherries should be served slightly chilled), and white and sparkling wine chilled.

Wines come in a variety of containers. Hundreds of bottles of wine from all over the world distinguish the collection available for your selection. Bottle sizes to suit every party, every taste and yes, every purse, are among your choices. Sizes and their approximate "yields" are:

Split bottles—2 glasses
Half bottles—3 glasses
Bottle—6 glasses (26 ounces) at 12 bottles/case = 72 drinks/case
Magnum—12 glasses (52 ounces) at 6 bottles/case = 72 drinks/case
Jeroboam—24 glasses (104 ounces), double magnum

What kind of glass should wine be served in? "Good wines need no bush," some pundit said

These are the two standard shapes of wine glasses

Different types of wine are poured to different levels in a glass

more than 2,000 years ago. However, good wine always did and always will need a glass in which it will look its best. It needs a glass that will show off its sweet bouquet and "come to our lips to that kiss of death for which it was born," according to enologist (wine expert) Andre L. Simon.

An all-purpose stemmed glass (including an 8-ounce champagne glass) is generally best for serving wine. This type glass will help the wine's "breathing" and develop its full bouquet and appearance, assuming the glass is not filled too full. Generally, it is best to use clear or colorless wine glasses.

Wine and Cheese Parties

An increasingly popular way to serve wine these days is through a wine-and-cheese-tasting party. The event is especially good, I think, for "promotional" events, such as a fund-raiser.

Much of my information on how to handle a first-class wine-and-cheese-tasting party comes from Winston J. Schuler, founder of the famed Schuler Restaurant chain. Mr. Schuler was our house guest following a recent nationwide wine-and-cheese tour.

I came to know and admire Mr. Schuler as one of the industry's all-time greats when I was a student at the Hotel and Restaurant Management School at Michigan State University. He has been involved with the MSU dairy department for years and has successfully merchandised not only his own cheese, but others as well.

Incidentally, don't for a moment feel uncomfortable serving "domestic" cheeses. Fine cheeses—patterned after such European greats as Camembert and Brie—are being turned out today in Michigan, Illinois, and Wisconsin. Certainly, we as consumers save the import tax and expensive transportation costs by purchasing the United States products.

A wine-and-cheese party is great not only for a promotion or fund-raiser, but for many other occasions. Schuler suggests sending out a simple invitation, something like this:

Come for
Cheese and Wine
from
Six Until Nine

How do you go about organizing a wine-and-cheese-tasting party? I suggest you enlist the aid of a local wine dealer. He or she can help you set up your party and help serve the wine to boot. Further, he might be able to furnish printed materials, video presentations, and display props, such as tables, corks, bottles (all sizes and kinds), and maps.

Next, try to get your local newspaper's food editor to give you a plug. Most metropolitan areas today have a fine-wine and food editor. This person will probably have many contacts and ideas that can help you. Be sure to include

This is the type of setup you'll want to provide for after-dinner guests being treated to champagne and brandy. At this point, some light entertainment might be in order.

this person in your party—perhaps as a master of ceremonies.

Cheese is a natural with wine. Basic cheese can be improved by adding nuts, seeds, soya, and other health foods. Many are pliable and can be molded into designs, such as the shape of a state, for special effect.

You can have a cold rarebit by adding ale, beer, wine, port, sherry and a touch of Worcestershire, or curry-filled cheeses. Make it as thin or thick as you like. Basic salad dressings can also be added with filled cheeses for endless variations, for dips, molds or spreads. Also, cottage cheese can be used as an extender.

Good wines and good times go together. Shakespeare, for example, wrote of the *friendliness* of wine. And in the *Rubáiyát,* Omar Khayám painted a picture of *contentment* when he wrote, "A loaf of bread, a jug of wine, and thou."

Bar Check List

Following is a complete bar set-up list. I recommend using it as a "reminder" list. Obviously, everything here is not necessary for every set-up.

Bar Fruit
- Oranges
- Limes
- Lemon twists
- Cherries
- Olives
- Cocktail onions

Mixes
- Club soda
- Tonic water
- Cola
- Lemon-Lime
- Beef broth
- Tomato juice
- Orange juice
- Grapefruit juice
- Sweet and sour mix
- Ice

Seasonings
- Salt and pepper
- Nutmeg
- Worcestershire sauce
- Tabasco sauce
- Grenadine
- Dry vermouth
- Roses lime
- Simple syrup

Equipment
- Ice bucket
- 1 shot glass
- Bar spoons
- Can opener
- Strainer
- Water pitcher
- Stirrers
- Corkscrew
- Knife for bar fruit
- Small cutting board or marble slab

Supplies
- Wiping towels
- Napkins
- Glasses (depends on number of guests)
  - 2 basic kinds, tall and short;
- Wine
- Snifters
- Straws and toothpicks

Beverages
- Scotch
- Bourbon
- Gin
- Vodka
- Beer
- Soft drinks (including diet drinks)
- White wine
- Mineral and sparkling water

Ideas for Beverages to Serve

Punch Bowl Ice Ring

4 candied red cherries, halved
16 pieces angelica, 1 inch long
8 lemon or lime slices, 1/4 inch thick

Choose a ring mold that will fit your punch bowl; place it in freezer until well chilled. Use heart-shaped mold for wedding reception. Rinse inside of mold with cold water; return to freezer until thin coating of ice forms.

Arrange cherries rounded side down and evenly spaced, in bottom of mold. Place two pieces of angelica on each cherry, extending to resemble leaves.

Slowly add about 1/4 cup cold water, or just enough to cover the cherries slightly (too much water would dislodge fruit.) Freeze until firm.

Arrange lemon slices directly over cherries; add just enough cold water to cover slightly. Freeze until firm.

Fill mold to top with cold water; freeze until firm. When ready to use, run cold water over mold to loosen; unmold. Float ring on punch in bowl. Often, it is well to pour cups of punch ahead to maintain even traffic flow or at least avoid waiting line.

Cranberry Frost Recipe

1 can frozen cranberry juice
1 can frozen apple juice
$4\frac{1}{2}$ cans chopped ice

Blend to a smooth but not melted consistency, like a frappé. Serve with straws in a pretty stemmed glass. (Long straws may be cut to appropriate sizes.) Garnish with fresh mint sprig. You may make this in advance and put in your freezer. Remember to take it out in time for it to soften enough to scoop into the glasses.

This is a great drink for Christmas, Valentine's Day, July 4th, or for any party year round. It is colorful, refreshing, healthful and lasts a long time, which means you won't run yourself to death for refills. Your guests will love it.

Melon Cooler
(serves 6)

1 small cantaloupe
1 can crushed pineapple (1 lb. $4\frac{1}{2}$ oz.)
12 cubes ice
sparkling water

Peel and seed cantaloupe; cut fruit into chunks. Blend cantaloupe, pineapple, and ice at high speed until smooth. Pour glasses $\frac{2}{3}$ full; add sparkling water and stir. Add sliced thin lime with fresh mint to garnish.

Spiced Tea Recipe
(For added flavor, make at least 24 hours in advance.)

This is inexpensive, easy and delicious. Makes about 40 cups. Serve hot or cold with fresh mint and orange wedge to garnish. In a large pot add:

16 tablespoons instant iced tea mix, low calorie, lemon flavored
2 gallons water
4 teaspoons nutmeg
3 tablespoons whole cloves
10 whole cinnamon sticks (broken in half)
$1\frac{1}{2}$ teaspoons ground ginger

Cover and simmer 1 hour. Let cool and add two 46-ounce cans pineapple juice, $1\frac{1}{2}$ quarts cranberry juice, or $1\frac{1}{2}$ quarts apple juice. (A good combination is half cranberry and half apple juice.) This will keep in the refrigerator for a week. The aroma is enticing.

Quick, Easy Eggnog

Vanilla ice cream softened, with bourbon and nutmeg added makes a delightful drink.

Surprise Cappuccino
(For after dinner or in place of dessert.)

1 cup coffee
1 cup of hot chocolate
2 ounces Galliano
1 teaspoon grated orange peel
dash of nutmeg
whipped cream

Combine hot chocolate and coffee. Add Galliano, grated orange peel, and nutmeg. Stir and pour into demitasse cups. Top with whipped cream and serve. Serves 4 demitasse.

And finally, remember:

1. Be yourself.
2. Be ready. (There is no substitute for planning and advanced preparation.)
3. Be happy. Make decisions quickly.
4. "Do unto others as you would have them do unto you."

Happy parties,

Index